EAGLE INSTINCTS

EAGLE INSTINCTS

The 7 Eagle Laws Every Leader Knows

DALLAS GATES MCCLAIN

XULON PRESS

Xulon Press
2301 Lucien Way #415
Maitland, FL 32751
407.339.4217
www.xulonpress.com

Xulon
PRESS

Paperback ISBN-13: 978-1-66286-100-0
Ebook ISBN-13: 978-1-66286-101-7

A Special Reminder

Before we jump into this book, it's my desire to make one think clear. Without having a special relationship with God, the rules I'm sharing will not be of any service to you. Yes, you may become rich and, yes, you may become very successful, but it won't matter unless you have a close connection with the Lord. Many people search all over this world for something to satisfy them. They go east and west and north and south. They get involved in all types of things, trying to find that one thing that gets them up in the morning. The meaning of life, right? What these people do not realize is that nothing except a personal, firm relationship with God can fill that empty void. Only God's love can fill one's heart with the necessary satisfaction and happiness to fully enjoy life.

I have read many books about personal development, and only the best of them mention the necessity of having a spiritual connection with God in order to succeed here on Earth and, more importantly, on the stairway to heaven. (Go crazy Led Zeppelin fans.) Most of the self-help books out there don't reference God or religion whatsoever. What many of these authors do not realize is that everything good they are writing about comes from God and His love. The Bible is the Book of all books because it teaches us the difference between right and wrong. It teaches us love and strength. From it stems all the other information on goodness that is discussed today. The information has, of course, been broken down and written in a way that's easier to understand, but it is still a descendant from God's Word and we need to continually remind ourselves of this.

Maybe many of the self-help book authors don't mention God in their material because of the fear of offending someone or hurting their profits. The fact of the matter is that God exists, and if that offends someone, then so be it. Sometimes taking offense to something is the first reaction on the journey to change. If we stay still in order to not offend, then is this not living out of fear? My advice is to believe what you believe, and (respectfully) say what you feel regardless of the fact that it may offend others. Let us not forget we are all brothers and sisters, created by the same hand of life. For this reason, despite our differences, we must learn to love, to be loved, and to grow to expand our perspectives of understanding.

God said we cannot serve two masters. We cannot serve both God and money. Yet, many people, myself included sometimes, tend to be a slave to money and all that it provides. Yet Jesus has repeatedly told us that there is no point to worrying and that the Lord will provide for us. We only have to first serve and worship Him and then He will provide all of our earthly needs. We must have complete faith in the Lord our God and never hold other idols above Him. Other idols can include many things, even those we love, such as parents, spouses, and children. To follow Christ faithfully and be the light of the world, we must learn to accept the idea that these people, these relatives of ours, are in actuality not our belongings. They are children of God and, for this reason, we must not confide all of our faith and love in them because if we do, then when they pass away, we pass with them. We must put all of our faith in God so that we can learn to love unconditionally like Jesus Christ; then we can pass this love on to our loved ones.

We must recognize everything in our lives is a gift from God, and without the Lord, it is impossible to live. For this reason, it is absolutely necessary to put God before anything else in our lives, even our own family. In this way, we can have a pure, faithful heart which cannot become shaken by difficult times, one that does not harness fear or worry. We have faith by knowing there is eternal life. This frees us from the fear of suffering and the fear of death. This gives us the ability to "die" for one another and, most importantly, to die for Christ. There is nothing to fear because Christ has conquered death. Have faith that there is eternal life and that it will be given to you. Then you can move through life free from worry and fear, able to serve your loved ones and enemies alike, with unconditional love and grace.

This reading from the gospel of Luke is perhaps the best advice Jesus has ever given us. It reads as follows according to the New Jerusalem Bible:

> A man in the crowd said to him, "Master, tell my brother to give me a share of our inheritance." He said to him, "My friend, who appointed me your judge, or the arbitrator of your claims?" Then he said to them, "Watch, and be on your guard against avarice of any kind, for life does not consist in possessions, even when someone has more than he needs." Then he told them a parable, "There was once a rich man who, having had a good harvest from his land, thought to himself, 'What am I to do? I have not enough room to store my crops.' Then he said, 'This is what I will do: I will pull down my barns and build bigger ones, and store all my grain and my goods in them, and I will say to my soul: My soul, you have plenty of good things laid by for many years to come; take things easy, eat, drink, have a good time.' But God said to him, 'Fool! This very night the demand will be made for your soul; and this hoard of yours, whose will it be then?' So it is when someone stores up treasure for himself instead of becoming rich in the sight of God." Then he said to his disciples, 'That is why I am telling you not to worry about your life and what you are to eat, nor about your body and how you are to clothe it. For life is more than food, and the body more than clothing. Think of the ravens. They do not sow or

reap; they have no storehouses and no barns; yet God feeds them. And how much more you are worth than the birds! Can any of you, however much you worry, add a single cubit to your span of life? If a very small thing is beyond your powers, why worry about the rest? Think how the flowers grow; they never have to spin or weave; yet, I assure you, not even Solomon in all his royal robes was clothed like one of them. Now if that is how God clothes a flower which is growing wild today and is thrown into the furnace tomorrow, how much more will he look after you, who have so little faith! But you must not set your hearts on things to eat and things to drink; nor must you worry. It is the gentiles of this world who set their hearts on all these things. Your Father well knows you need them. No; set your hearts on his kingdom, and these other things will be given you as well.' Luke 12; 13-34[1]

Life is not meant for man to work like a slave to accumulate money in vast amounts only to store it for a long time. It's alright to make money and be rich, but it's important that you don't let your money sit idle lest it become your master and control your life. Put your resources to use. Make them work for you. Invest. Donate. Create something. We are not meant to be couch potatoes in the physical sense as well as in the spiritual sense. We have to strive to continue to grow our relationship with God. When we only live to serve money, we make it our master and we dismiss God, even though God is the only one who makes our life possible in the first place. Instead of storing our riches and rotting our lives away, we should be adventurous and explore the world and the opportunities it has to offer by being open to the responsible spending of our resources.

---

[1] https://www.bibliacatolica.com.br/new-jerusalem-bible/luke/12/

Choose to serve God and let Him worry about the provisions. He will provide. Worrying will not add anything to your life but stress and discomfort. Let it go and give all your worries to the Lord. It is important to work and create; God knows this. For that reason, He encourages us to work well and happily; It is alright to make money through our work. But just like with our affection towards our loved ones, we cannot let work consume us. When it consumes us, we go where it goes and we become slaves to it. Think about the 2008 economic crisis. So many people who built their companies and made their fortunes before that year couldn't stand to have all their possessions and money taken away from them, so, they fell into a great depression and let money control their emotions. Some even let money take their lives through suicide.

This is what the devil wants. He wants us to serve other things, like money, family, friends, sex, alcohol, drugs, etc. These are many things that are indeed good and pleasurable to have. It's okay to have healthy associations with these things, but when we begin to serve them and sacrifice our time and worship with God for them, we become slaves and forget that without God none of these things would exist. They are all presents from God. We have to have the courage and unwavering faith to put God first, over everything else, so we can better serve the Lord and the world.

Do you see how this establishes one to be a better person? By serving the Lord faithfully, we learn how to serve the world faithfully and graciously share our talents and services. Jesus said the best leaders are those who serve. It is through the service of others that we are able to lead. This is important to remember when thinking about personal development. The question is not how will I make money. No, the question is how will I better serve my fellow brothers and sisters. When you find your way to serve and contribute, the proper payment will be provided unto you.

Now maybe you are not a Christian. Maybe you are not a monotheistic believer. Maybe you aren't even a spiritual person. Know that

I still love you as my neighbor because I am a follower of Christ and His teachings. In the same way, I write this book without fear of criticism from those who believe and don't believe because I have faith that, through Jesus Christ, my words will touch someone and help them find their way toward God. Even if it is only one person out of a thousand, it will be a blessing; it will still change the world.

I'm not saying that you have to be a Christian, and you don't have to claim a denomination, but I believe you do have to believe in something greater than yourself; something that gives everything the breath and miracle of life, something that makes the world go around. You do have to be a believer in order to grow. Without belief, there is no hope for worthy change. But with belief, there is hope for not only worthy but *worldly* change.

One last note here for all those who may harden their hearts to this message on account of their past. We have all done things we are not proud of. We have a tendency to try and separate ourselves from these dark periods in our lives and free ourselves from the reputation they portray. In reality, we must act like Christ and embrace these experiences and carry them with us, like Jesus carried the cross. We can act differently and be better people, but only after recognizing these experiences helped take us to where we are today, and that with humility, we can ask for forgiveness in order to free us from the power of shame. God is merciful because He loves us. When we pray with humility and forgiveness, we become more capable of loving like Christ loves. Our past mistakes do not define us, but they do shape us. Accepting this and finding the strength from God to forgive ourselves and others allows us to purely and freely do the one thing we all were born to do—love. Let us remember this verse from Psalms 103: 1-5:

> Bless Yahweh, my soul, from the depths of my being,
> his holy name; bless Yahweh, my soul, never forget all
> his acts of kindness. He forgives all your offences, cures
> all your diseases, he redeems your life from the abyss,

crowns you with faithful love and tenderness; he contents you with good things all your life, renews your youth like *an eagle's.* [2]

God bless you all, and pray for me as I pray for you. Amen.

---

[2] https://www.bibliacatolica.com.br/new-jerusalem-bible/psalms/103/

TABLE OF CONTENTS

INTRODUCTION

The aguila. The erne. The raptor in the sky. The bird of Jove. This soaring beauty goes by many names and has been deemed the mightiest creature in the sky. Most know it best as the eagle. With its glorious wings and fierce stare, the eagle has long been considered a reverent symbol in the sky by humankind. Some might even say that eagles resemble angels of God, flying high over the land to keep watch over all of us. Of course, in this age, we can scientifically conclude that an eagle belongs to the animal kingdom and that, of course, as an animal, it has instincts. But what makes an eagle's instincts so important to its survival and places it at the top of the sky? eagles instinctually know the ways of life, the laws of the land, the unwritten rules that carry it toward the ceilings of light and success. Like an eagle, you must instinctually know these laws in order to rise above the troposphere and soar like a champion in the unpredictable breeze of life.

No, this book isn't all about eagles or birds of prey. (Sorry, bird lovers.) What you will find in this book are simple, clear, and concise guidelines to prepare you for the world ahead. There is a reason the bald eagle in particular has stood as the national emblem of the United States from the country's beginning and also has been a spiritual symbol for native people for far longer. Its cultural meaning is just as vital to our understanding of its mysteriousness, which elevates this great species to a lofty height of respect and admiration. I reference the eagle partially because it's a great icon of power and beauty but also, and perhaps primarily, because of its widely known status as the top rank in the Boy Scouts of America.

The Boy Scouts organization helps prepare young men to live off the land, work together in harmony, and lead with vision and understanding. And these are just some of the main lessons it imparts. There are countless more that are gained from various merit badges, ranging from Citizenship in the Word to Lifesaving or Emergency Preparedness. Whatever the subject is, you can almost guarantee there's a merit badge handbook ready to teach eager learners.

There is one branch of learning, though, that has not yet been stitched into the sash of the scout uniform. It's commonly called personal development. The lack of its inclusion could be for many reasons: it's too much information to learn in one sitting, those given the knowledge aren't sure how to teach it, or maybe it's just so rare that almost no one thinks to add it to the common curriculum. Whatever the reason, it is clear to say there is little to no emphasis on this field of learning in the Boy Scout handbook. Perhaps the timing isn't quite right.. After all, a boy ought to enjoy his childhood and not spend too much time learning and studying. Well, if we grant this argument passage, then it is more than appropriate to say that when a boy is on the edge of manhood and has achieved the rank of Eagle Scout, he is ready to open the door to this field of education.

Personal Development is at the true essence of defining and refining your character for the better. Without it, the world would have no leaders to inspire change and progress. It's the most important thing you can or could ever invest in, and if you're lucky, it comes to you at an ideal time in your life, like when becoming an Eagle Scout for example.

In my case, I didn't find out about this life-changing gateway of education until I was well past my Eagle Scout ceremony. Don't get me wrong, I learned and still carry many great ideals and mentalities from my time as a Boy Scout, such as the Scout Law ("A Scout is trustworthy, loyal, helpful, friendly, courteous, kind, obedient, cheerful, thrifty, brave, clean, and reverent"). I am in no way demeaning my Scouting background; quite the opposite. I learned many great qualities and cornerstones of what makes a good leader, and I also found solid relationship-building fundamentals that would help me for many years to come. I am only saying that if there had been a separate course, badge, or project geared toward personal development that came during or immediately after my journey to an Eagle Scout, perhaps I would have saved myself from a history of ups and downs, and developed a clearer sense of life at an earlier age. Let me explain my story in a bit more detail.

I was raised in the nurturing foothills of North Carolina, a state I now only see on holidays. I came from a middle-class family that taught me manners with a dash of southern chivalry. Although my parents divorced when I was a teenager, my sister and I had pretty normal childhoods (depending on your definition of normal). The stock market crash of 2008 happened when I was in eleventh grade, and I remember all the adults in my life being glued to the television. At the time, I didn't really find any interest behind the upheaval; I had stuff figured out already, just like any over-confident seventeen-year old. My A and B grades in high school got me into a pretty good university where I was introduced to the infamous college party atmosphere. The lifestyle overtook me. I saw alcohol and marijuana more as "friends" than study-halls and homework. This eventually got me to the point where I almost got kicked out of school for violating alcohol-related, "dry-law" policies...three separate times...in a year. It is safe to say that in my freshman year I was losing sleep, finding trouble, and out of control.

Even after a rough freshman year, my GPA was still salvageable. I turned my act around and focused my attention a bit more on my classes. However, I was still going out and having a good deal of fun . To counteract my party lifestyle, I crammed and studied every chance I could. As perilous as this strategy seemed, it worked to a degree, and I graduated college with a Bachelors in Biology with a 2.96 GPA.

Although I graduated, I had no internships lined up, no job interviews, and no plan.

The night of July 4th right after college ended was perhaps the worst night of my life. I was pulled over for speeding and later arrested for a DUI. I blew a .08 and I honestly thought I was fine to drive, so I took it to court. While I was waiting for the court date, I took all the necessary classes to create some mitigating factors to hopefully resolve the case in my favor. At this time, I was working at a GNC and because of all the added stress from the DUI charge, I decided I needed a change in my life. I had the same circle of friends, the same habits, and the same scene all around. So, I took a job from my uncle in Florida as a Training Coordinator for Westgate Resorts. In my mind, I knew I needed to lock myself away and escape my usual network of peers to really discover myself. When I got to Florida, my life slowly seemed to grow a little towards the positive side. After settling into my new job, I started to enjoy the company of the people around me. I was making favorable connections, solid friendships, and a decent living. The best new addition in my new environment came when a beautiful Colombian woman entered my world with a wide smile and a dashing glance. Her continual laughter and positive, child-like outlook made my worries almost fade away completely. From very early on, I knew I was in love.

As fulfilling as my life in the present was going, my past was still haunting me. The trial date back in North Carolina eventually came, and after two and a half years of waiting, the verdict was in. I was charged guilty by a jury of my peers. The district attorney pushed for me to have almost three months of jail time. Standing there, I prayed to God with more effort than I ever had. I felt everyone in the courtroom could hear my prayers echo outside of my head. Luckily, my prayers were answered and the judge sympathized with my situation. I had a full-time job in Florida, a very serious relationship; essentially a new home base. He gave me unsupervised probation for a year, a North Carolina license suspension for a year, fifty hours of community service, and some hefty court fines. I gladly accepted my punishment and went back to Florida smiling with tears in the corners of my eyes. It was finally over. I completed the community service quickly, volunteering in the hot Florida summer for a few weekends. At that point, I remember thinking about how blessed I truly was.

With the court case behind me, life jumped back to the present. I was sleeping much better, my hair stopped graying, and I finally felt like I could focus. I turned my attention to my still fresh job at Westgate. It was at this job where I met an interesting co-worker named Chris. He had an outlook on life different than most. We soon became good friends. One day we were discussing the subject of reading and I asked him to suggest a good book. He suggested *The Slight Edge* by Jeff Olson. I remember ordering it on Amazon that same day. Chris recommended I just commit to reading ten pages a day. Anyone could find time for that. I actually had to hold myself back from reading more than ten pages a day because this book had me hooked from the day I opened it. Each workday I would discuss the passages I'd read with Chris and he would counter with other perspectives. These insightful conversations opened my outlook on the world wider than I could have previously imagined.

After reading *The Slight Edge*, I asked if he could suggest the next book to read. And then the next…and the next… until today. At the time I am writing this, it has been more than three years since the beginning of my personal development journey, and I haven't stopped reading. I have read more than thirty books in the genre, all of which have impacted my life immensely.

In just three years, it is truly incomprehensible how much my life has improved. I am married to a beautiful, good-hearted woman; my finances have made a 360; I have learned how to dance salsa and speak Spanish; how to get closer to God; and how to better control my tendencies and influencing factors. Perhaps most importantly, I have learned to change my entire way of thinking, my entire philosophy of life. It is like putting glasses on after have blurred vision for so long. Things just seem much clearer. And the more I read, the clearer things, people, situations, and themes appear.

I know I have not been transformed into a perfect human being. I still make mistakes, plenty of them. However, now I believe I am able to look at my mistakes and learn more from them as opposed to before. Now I get a little excited when I make a mistake simply because of the learning-opportunity. Anyway, the point is that, although I am not perfect, I am better than I was three years ago, and I know I will be better than when I completed this sentence I am currently writing.

We only get one life, and we can't spend too much time analyzing what we could have or should have done. We can only reflect, learn, and adjust. But this book isn't about that and it isn't about me. It's about you. I wrote this book to help all aspiring men and women who have tasted the frosting of leadership from the BSA (or a similar organization focused on building leaders) but now want to discover the recipe for themselves so they can bake their own cake of success. I hope my words might save readers from making mistakes similar to mine, and save them valuable time away from worry and torment. This book was written to serve my fellow man. This is where you can start to change your thinking and live happily in sync with everything in the world.

This is the badge. This is the project. This is the course. With this book, you'll learn all the hidden rules of life that make the proud eagles soar the skies and capture the numerous field mice scurrying over life's perilous obstacles.

The process of growth requires humility. We can't expect to know everything. Our minds should always be open to learning something new and the opportunity to do so should never be seen as impossible. As Ralph Waldo Emerson put it, "Every man is my superior in some way. In that, I learn from him." Smugness and pride only cause others to resent us. Have the humbleness to admit when you don't know something and be eager to learn something new. This is the ideal way to become wise *and* respected.

And remember, enjoy the learning process. Tension and stress about learning the material only cloud the mind. Be open and let your mind have fun with it. As David Ogilvy, arguably the greatest ad man of all time once said, "When people aren't having any fun, they seldom produce good work."

Embrace your future and soar like the eagle.

-Dallas Gates McClain

Chapter 1

GETTING STARTED

Why am I reading this?

How can I apply it?

What will happen?

A h, the three main questions that go through any books skeptic's mind before turning another page with their dusty Cheetos fingers (okay maybe damp carrot-hands for all you health nuts; I'm with ya). It's great to ask questions. It's even better to ask the *right* questions; and its best if you ask the *right* questions in the *right* order. Throughout the book, we will be answering these questions in a similar fashion relating to each particular law. Our brain is more inclined to understand when we start asking these questions in this order. WHY and HOW are more emotional questions and come from our intuitive part of our brain. WHAT is more rational and logical. In order for true comprehension and understanding, the WHY behind the process must match with the output of the process itself, the WHAT. Best-selling author, Simon Sinek said it best with this statement: "A WHY is just a belief. That's all it is. HOWs are the actions you take to realize that belief. And WHATs are the results of those actions—everything you say and do." When we learn to start with WHY, we break the information down into pleasurable chunks of data that first appeal to our emotional side and then finishes with our logical side. So for this introduction, let's start with WHY.

I could be lazy or a jerk and just respond with another cliché question: "I don't know, why is the sky blue?" or "Why does your nose have gross boogers?" There's an endless supply of these (of questions, not boogers). The best answer to this question why is its opposite; why not? Why not read this this book? You are here for a reason. Something or someone caused the universe to conspire and put this book in your hands. And so here you are. Are you really going to try and deny the universe of its desires to help you excel? I think not.

The point I'm trying to make is that you are here for a reason. You are on this Earth for a reason, for a purpose. Now, that purpose doesn't always show itself on a bright display every Sunday morning after brunch and orange juice Most of the time, you have to go searching for it. You have to look deep down into your soul and find that burning desire to make your dream a reality. In order to begin this process, you have to be open to knowledge that was designed to serve you; in other words, you have to have the awareness to capitalize on the opportunities the universe throws your way. This book could be that opportunity that sheds light on a whole new set of unawaken goals and possibilities. Why not read the following chapters and then make the call on what information to keep and what to discard. It's your life. It's your mind. Don't just blindly follow any information that comes your way, though. That would be foolish. Instead, be a curious observer who takes notes on what he likes and then moves on with his life, applying what he feels is best. That's the best rhythm to learn to; one with your own beat and pace. Best-selling author, Robert Green had a nice way of writing about the learning process: "Your whole life is a kind of apprenticeship to which you apply your learning skills. Everything that happens to you is a form of instruction if you pay attention."

And now for the second question: How can I apply it?

Well, the best way to apply something is to start practicing it in small, incremental steps. Take a diet for example. You've researched a whole new diet plan that is going to get you into shape before summer. Great. You decide to go cold turkey and finally after two weeks you cave and buy the ice cream. What happened? Most of us know by now that quitting something you're habitually used to is not easy, especially going cold turkey with anything that has highly addictive properties, such as sugar or cigarettes. The best way to implement a new habit is to gradually introduce it into your lifestyle. For example, instead of quitting cold turkey, why not try to eat five healthy meals out of the week. That's it. That's all you have to do. Focus on that. Then adjust when you feel comfortable. Create the discomfort to create the change. Move it to ten healthy meals a week next. And so on and so on. Don't fool yourself, however. Have the determination and awareness to know when you're in your comfort zone and when it's time to add another challenge to promote growth.

These *eagle* rules work the same way. Read them, study them, ponder them. And then try to apply them to small areas of your life. Keep them in the back of your mind as you go about your daily routine. Ask yourself, am I able to reference a rule here? If you are ready, try it and see how it goes. When you think you've got the hang of it, look at some other, perhaps more significant, areas of your life and gauge where you can see some potential for growth if you apply the same rule.

And now the question most people focus on—the WHAT. What will happen?

This is what most people want to know right off the bat. We live in the information age, and everyone is in a rush to get the results in the same time it takes to get a cup of chili at Wendy's. Yes, I like Wendy's chili, but is it as good as grandma's chili that has been slowly cooking for hours on end on the stove top? Not a chance Wendy's, not a chance.

What you will get from this book is a set of rules that most of the world doesn't know about; or worse, some people know about them but are too careless to do anything with them. Don't let this be you. These laws are the same followed by all those who make it to the top in life. It is worth noting that it is almost never a quick hike to the peak of the mountain. It takes patience and continual, gradual investment to reach the summit.

From this point forward, consider yourself in a different class of students. Students who never stop the learning process. Students who persevere toward the achievement of a worthy goal. Students who have earned the right to call themselves the eagles of the World. Once you grow this power inside of you, do not be surprised if your usual circle of friends alters on account of unsupportiveness. Paulo Coelho, author of *The Alchemist*, warned us of this fact when he wrote "When you possess great treasures within you, and try to tell others of them, seldom are you believed." After reading this book and other personal development teachings, if you're like me, you'll become so excited to share the information with people you know and even suggest books to those you want to see succeed. My advice is to focus first on applying the principles you've learned on yourself, then let the results of your continued practice speak for themselves. This way those in your life who are interested will ask, and you can share your knowledge knowing it is welcome. Still, while you're learning this type of stuff, it gets you very motivated and excited, understandably so. I suggest you find a mentor or someone who is interested in the same type of reading. Share what you've read with them and enjoy the experience of putting all of those wondering thoughts into words of fruitful expression. It will help organize your mind so that you can fill it with more helpful knowledge.

By reading this book and applying these *eagle* laws, I can promise you that you'll see results, but I can also promise you that they won't be instant. That doesn't mean put the book down and go get a donut with crème filling. It means that results actually worth something take time to achieve and master. With constant learning and by revisiting these laws often, you'll start to see your life change from the inside out, beginning with your thoughts, and then your attitude, and then your actions. Then, and only then, will you start to see the results. Then these laws will slowly fuse with your habit and become *eagle* instincts. Revisit this book after reading it and commit yourself to the information. Treat it like gold or riches! Realize some are not so lucky to have this information so readily available to them. Remember that a man's property and wealth can be taken from him, but as long as he has his mind, he can easily create more riches. Information is what creates things. It all starts in your head. The key is to put so much personal development information into that brain of yours that there is nowhere to go but up.

Without further ado, turn the page to discover the laws that every true eagle knows.

Chapter 2

THE LAW OF TIME

Disciplined Choices Now = Successful Rewards Later

> "We are what we repeatedly do. Excellence, then, is not
> an act, but a habit." – Aristotle

Try this exercise. Go outside on partly cloudy day and pick one cloud to watch for a couple of minutes. See if you can track how it changes shape, the direction it moves, the shifts in its color. I think you'll find this exercise is much more difficult than it seems.

Clouds are constantly changing, and it's almost impossible to note every single detail. Clouds are my chosen object because they display some of the changes nature shows us every day in a time frame we can physically see in the moment. Still, it's near impossible to track the detail of every single little change. Most of the magnificent and remarkable elements nature has made have taken countless years to form. Mountains, valleys, rivers—all of these represent a product that has been made by small forces of nature acting upon it over a long amount of time. These forces, although seemingly ineffective when observed in the small fraction of a moment, add up to create a huge step in the formation of these respective landmarks. Contrary to cloud formation, landmarks are formed over longer periods of time and involve many small changes which contribute to the look and shape we see today.

How does this relate to you? Well, humans, whether we accept it or not, are subject to these same forces of nature. In fact, we are able to harness this same force for our own betterment as a species and as individuals. Most people call this force "discipline." We use discipline to make decisions that will either hurt us or help us. The tricky thing is that when we make a decision, the effects aren't shown to us immediately, unlike the change in the shape of a cloud. Instead, we start to see the results of most of these decisions long after the moment has passed, just like the slow erosion of a river bank or the rising of the ocean levels. The beautiful structures on Earth were not made with the swipe of a paint brush. They were brought to life with carefully chosen and coordinated brush strokes, which in turn illustrate the immense amount of detail and work that was put into its creation. We don't notice this at first glance, but when we stare deeper into a painting, we come to understand the continual focus and discipline that went into its creation.

Now, back to you. Let's start asking some questions. First, why should you have the discipline to make better choices? The answer can be best explained by looking at your future years down the road. Do you want to end up in a rocking chair in a nursing home, taking God knows how much medication due to poor health choices, relying on others and the government to support you due to poor financial choices, and not having any close friends or family due to poor relationship choices? This is the sad reality for many people, and they wonder why. It all begins with something as small as a decision in the present moment.

But another question presents itself here. Why does a huge change start with small choices? Well, respectfully, where else would you start? When we want to change something, we have to begin by looking at our simple daily actions, which we have free choice over. These are the building blocks of the structure we aim to build. Now, based off the types of choices we continually make over time, we either supply ourselves with strong, sturdy steel and construct a skyscraper that towers into the sky, built on a solid foundation of good choice or we built a little shack that shivers at the sight of rain and touch of wind, built sloppily in a ditch flowing with a stream of bad choices. The reason why we have to start with small choices to create a big change is because valuable things take time to build. The builders don't start at the top of the building and concern themselves with decisions that will be made months of years from now. They start building from the ground up and focus on what they know they can do now. Through these initial choices, they can then move up level by level and make new, more challenging decisions based off their past choices. Slowly but surely, they'll have built an impressive structure that stands proud in the sky. And it all started with the choice at the foundation, the decision to break ground with something as simple as a shovel. Start with your shovel. Start with what you know. Then move up to working with the hammer. Follow that with the wrench, and finally, the crane. It's by starting small that we show the world and our fellow inhabitants that we have learned to be responsible with what we have, and in turn they will welcome us to the next level of growth. Although the next level may appear challenging and unknown, we are better prepared to make the proper choices because we will have proved ourselves by building a well-rounded, secure foundation.

One more question that concerns the WHY: Why do we have to wait? Why can't we just imagine something we want and then get it in one or two steps, or even instantly. I think after some internal reflection you would agree with me when I say there would be little to no satisfaction in life if all of our desires and wishes were gratified instantly. There is a natural cycle in life, one that determines how much we receive based off how much we give. The late, great American author and Hall-of-Fame speaker, Earl Nightingale describes the formula as such: "What we receive in life is in exact proportion to the amount of contribution we give, our service." When we work slowly over time towards a certain goal or objective, the reward is so much sweeter when we arrive. Think about when you bake a pie versus when you buy one. When you go through the entire process of rolling the dough and mixing the filling, you feel much more excited and prouder to enjoy the end result, the delicious pie. When you buy a pie, although the taste may be as satisfying, the sensation is gone quickly and there is not much of a story to tell afterward. When you make the pie yourself, you add some new content to your character and give yourself and the world something special: a story.

Now that you know why, let's move on to the HOW. How will you develop discipline? The easiest way is to use your Eagle Vision. It is estimated that an eagle's eyesight is four to eight times stronger than a human's. These birds can see their prey or their goal from up to two miles (3.2 kms) away.[3] This keeps them focused. This keeps them on course instead of changing direction at the sight of any meaningless distraction. Similarly, you have to set goals and keep them in your line of vision. Don't just say what you want. Write it down. Post it to your bathroom mirror so you see it every day when you wake up and go to sleep. You need to reserve an influential seat for your objective at your brain's conference table. By doing this, you'll not be as easily tempted in those defining moments of decision. You must develop the discipline to see through those everyday choices and picture how you will feel in the future after making those choices. If instant gratification is your game, you will find yourself lost in a world of dead dreams and regret. By subjecting yourself forcefully to your goals every day, you'll habitually make choices that serve to get you closer and closer to your dream. Because you are constantly refining the strength of your focus, you are constantly preparing yourself for life's great challenges, which unfailingly come to test the validity of our desires.

Now for the WHAT: What will change after I develop discipline? The answer is everything will change. The iconic speaker and business man Jim Rohn once said, "If you will change, everything will change for you." Once you develop discipline, you will see that because you yourself have changed, the whole world that surrounds you will change. Most people blame their position in life on outside forces. "I can't go

---

[3]*Grambo, Rebecca L. (14 December 2003). <u>eagles</u>. Voyageur Press. <u>ISBN 978-0-89658-363-4</u>.*

to school because it's raining," "I'm broke because the government takes too much money," "I'm single because no one gets me." There's an excuse for everything, and you can bet that most people use hundreds of them to justify their situations in life. Successful people know they can only blame themselves if they succeed or fail. Don't play the blame game. Take accountability for your actions.

When discipline becomes your go-to way of thinking, the results you want can't help but follow. But you have to keep your eye on the prize and not let the distractions of others throw you off your game. Yes, it's tempting to go out with your friends or have a party, but what about that book you said you'd read tonight? Which choice will help you progress further toward your goal? If you have been reviewing your goals every day, the decision will be less difficult. You'll have the discipline to say, "Hey I'd love to but I gotta study a bit and then maybe I'll catch up with you guys." It's okay to have some fun. You don't have to be a hermit. Just learn to set goals, have the discipline to steer your way around obstacles, and let time do the rest. When you work on yourself first and then go out for some fun, you'll realize the sense of satisfaction will feel that much more deserved.

An unfortunate few try to force time into impossible circumstances. Get rich quick schemers, gamblers, and lottery players fall into this category. Time doesn't work like that. Yes, some people win, but what usually happens is that they lose it all. Do you know why? That's right, they have not learned the discipline to handle it all. You value something a lot more when you earn it and work for it. When it's given to you by mere luck or chance, you have the tendency to be reckless and careless with it. It's only human nature. Remember the expression that Rome was not built in a day? As cliché as it sounds, it's true. Things of value take time to build, including strong relationships, a healthy body, and a secure financial position. Everything worth something that you have in your life took time to become what it is today.

An eagle is not born with the crucial flying ability that defines it as a dominant species. Take the rarest bird of prey in the world, the

Philippine eagle, for example. Although the chick is born with admirable wings, its flying muscles are weak and underdeveloped, making it completely dependent on its mother and father for food and survival. At four months old, it's already an impressive one meter tall, with a wingspan of two meters. As time goes on, the frequent food drops made by the mother and father become less frequent, and the chick's growing hunger pushes it towards growth. It begins to flap its wings in the nest, strengthening its once dormant flying muscles little by little. Then, the aspiring flyer begins to inch away from the security of its nest, using its talons to carefully grip the high tree branches as it side-steps over the jungle's forest floor; a death-drop of seventy meters. The young eagle is aware of the danger, but it knows that in order to grow, it must take uncomfortable risks by taking little steps every day outside of its comfort zone. Finally, one day, the adventurer's confidence level syncs with its muscle gain and it takes its first flight from the nesting tree. It will be a full year before the young eagle is completely independent, but its small, incremental steps began its vital transformation from chick to thriving adult eagle;[4] a transformation that will continue over its entire lifespan. The eagle's wings and flying ability will increase and become stronger as it gains experience. First, it will begin hunting for small prey it can carry without too much strain on its balance and wing-strength. Slowly but surely, it will work its way up to the larger prey, carrying back large carcasses with confidence and vigor. An eagle knows its greatest virtue of all has no set price. It cannot buy this skill of flight. Only by using the Law of Time combined with the discipline to take the right steps can the eaglet propel itself into the sky toward achievement and glory.

Many people often place most of their value on things that have a price. Material things like houses, cars, carpets, etc. These things, as nice as they are, are much less valuable than the things in our life that have no price, such as family, friends, and memories. These emotional

---

[4]"Our Planet" – Composed by Steven Price and Narrated by David Attenborough; Network: Netflix; Produced in Partnership with the World Wildlife Fund. 2019.

values come into our lives freely and have no set price, and as such, sometimes we tend to not value them as highly as the things that cost money. This is a dangerously slippery slope. When we put more value on material objects than our natural relationships with God, family, and friends, we enter into a world of endless greed and haunting guilt-iness. Better to know instead that with the support of God, family, and friends we can acquire material things as we wish and, should we lose them suddenly, lean on our support system to acquire them again. This doesn't work the other way around. Money doesn't buy happiness, and all the fine expensive things in the world won't buy love back from God, family, or friends. These relationships are priceless because they take time to build; after valiant effort, the returns from these relationships are tenfold. Develop the discipline to set the priority of God, family, and friends over life's so-called "finer" things.

When your friends and family notice your change in choices, they will wonder why. Some will cite evidences as to why you shouldn't be making certain choices. They do this because of fear. Watching you make good choices puts greater pressure on them to make similar deci-sions they may not yet be comfortable making. Thus, they come up with reasons why you shouldn't make that choice. The reality is their pressure will give way to one of three possible outcomes. One, you give into the pressure and resume making your normal choices even though you know it's not good for you. Two, the person gives in to your deter-mination and starts to make good choices as well. This is the ideal out-come. And three, you both go your separate ways because your paths are now in opposite directions. You are walking towards a healthier, better you, and they are heading to a stressful and unpleasant future. It's hard to hang out with someone who doesn't value the same principles. Know that we are a sum of the five people we spend most of our time with. Make sure you are spending time with those who are supportive and helping you achieve your goal, not those hindering or belittling you.

Letting friends go their separate ways is never easy. I had a friend in high school (let's call him Tim) who helped me learn to enjoy life a little more and let my extroverted side shine a bit brighter. I was a very shy kid all the way up until my last year of high school. I got a job at a veterinary hospital as a kennel attendant, and it was here that I met Tim. He was a funny, hard-working guy and we soon became good buddies. I started hanging out with him more on the weekends, and I was becoming more social in my school as well. As sociable and likable as Tim was, he also introduced me to a more alcoholic and narcotic lifestyle. I soon found myself getting into trouble with the law because of this new lifestyle I picked up. Still, I remained friends with him, even when my family and other friends told me countless times that Tim was a bad influence. I was blind because he was my closet friend at the time, and I didn't want to believe that he was getting me into trouble. I didn't want to believe this because I didn't want to choose the more difficult path and stop associating with him. Tim helped me greatly develop my social skills and also showed me a whole other culture (Tim was Vietnamese and I'm white, very white). As great as these things were though, they didn't outweigh the consequences I was experiencing by associating with him.

I eventually decided I had to cut him loose, and I stopped talking to him altogether. It wasn't easy at first, but as the weeks and months passed, I slowly began to see the effects of my decision to disassociate. There were times when I was really tested, tempted to contact Tim out of boredom or curiosity, but with God's strength, I held strong and refrained. It helped to remind myself that only I was in complete control of who I wanted to be around. I knew time would tell how long and how happy I lived largely based off of my closet group of friends. As tough as it was to remove one of my best friends from my life completely, I knew, in order to move up in life, I had to make the decision to accept the lessons I'd learned from Tim with appreciation and then move on. Some people will be in your life for almost forever and others will only last for a season or two. That's just the way it works. But I firmly believe that no matter how long someone is in our life, we have the opportunity to learn something from them.

I once read a metaphor about family and friends that really made me think. It was from a Tyler Perry movie and the character was the infamous Medea. She said,

> Some people are meant to come into your life for a lifetime, some for only a season, and you got to know which is which. And you're always messing up when you mix those seasonal people up with lifetime expectations. I put everybody that comes into my life in the category of a tree. Some people are like leaves on a tree. When the wind blows, they're over there…wind blow that way, they over here…they're unstable. When the seasons change, they wither and die, they're gone. That's alright. Most people are like that, they're not there to do anything but take from the tree and give shade every now and then. That's all they can do. But don't get mad at people like that, that's who they are. That's all they were put on this earth to be. A leaf. Some people are like a branch on that tree. You have to be careful with those branches too, 'cause they'll fool you. They'll make you think they're a good friend and they're real strong, but the minute you step out there on them, they'll break and leave you high and dry. But if you find two or three people in your life that's like the roots at the bottom of that tree you are blessed. Those are the kind of people that aren't going nowhere. They aren't worried about being seen, nobody has to know that they know you, they don't have to know what they're doing for you. But if those roots weren't there, that tree couldn't live. A tree could have a hundred million branches but it only takes a few roots down at the bottom to make sure that tree gets everything it needs. When you get some roots, hold on to them, but the rest of it…just let it go. Let folks go.

We have to learn to recognize who in our social circle is nourishing us like a tree root. This takes discipline. The discipline to notice each and every time that person is there for you. We should never make assumptions, but we can tread lightly sometimes to save ourselves from falling on our face when a "friend" lets us down. In other words, be open and loving to all, but be wary not to become attached to someone who is only making your life toxic. Develop the discipline to choose to be around those friends who encourage you to launch toward your dreams. Sometimes when you explain your dream to those that love you most, they will discourage you. Do not be upset with them; simply recognize they are only acting out of your best interest (as they perceive it). They may fear for your security or social acceptance, or maybe they just don't believe in you. That's alright. Because many times these people are family, it's possible to still have them in your life while you continue following your dream. In time, most of them will come to accept your vocation if you show the discipline to persist despite their influence.

Even an eagle knows when there is a "bad egg". As much as it may hurt, the sacrifice taken to remove the egg from the nest is minuscule compared to the unweighted flight potential that its removal invokes. With your associations properly balanced, you'll be able to live life with less exhaustion on account of not always having to defend your choices to someone; instead, you'll be encouraged. The road to your goal will be lined with cheering, instead of jeering.

In short, use your Eagle Vision to set your sights on a goal and move toward it every day by making the right decisions. This is how things change for the better. Simple, small steps in the right direction will lead you toward success. Remember that it can all be broken down into a choice in any given moment of your day. When presented with a decision, try to freeze the moment, and, picturing your goal, ask yourself if your choice will move you further away or pull your closer towards it. Time will continue to act regardless of how you choose. You can either have it work for you or against you. The decision is yours.

Chapter 3

THE LAW OF ATTRACTION

Adjusting your mind to work for you, rather than against you.

"The oak sleeps in the acorn. The bird waits in the egg,
and in the highest vision of the soul, a waking angel stirs.
Dreams are but seedlings of reality." – Napoleon Hill

Have you ever been thinking about a song while listening to the radio and all of the sudden the song comes on next? Crazy, right? Well, this is a great example of the Law of Attraction. It's been phrased in many different ways, but perhaps it can be said as simply this: what you think about, you attract. That's it. Expounding further, we can add that your conscious thoughts are eventually passed to your subconscious, where they are then communicated to the universe in order to manifest the thought in physical form into your life.

It's near impossible to have an eagle metaphor for this because, as humans, we are the only creatures on Earth that are able to use this law. Animals' minds are not on the same playing field. Looking at an animal's brain, the space between an animal's input and output are right next to each other. Because there is a direct path between the two, when an animal receives an input, there is an almost immediate output. Take the stimulus of food, for example. When a mouse has the input, of seeing food, it immediately connects to the output—eat food. There is not much time at all for it to think between the input and output. People, however, are able to see things differently. Using the food example, we, as humans, can of course eat the cheese it after seeing it, but we also can learn to control our initial instincts and use the food item as art, tools, or even expressions of disapproval (anyone who's had failures on stage knows the smell of rotten tomatoes all too well).

How are we able to do this? How are we able to be creative with something so basic to our survival as food? The answer can be found by looking at the difference in our brain structure. During the evolution of our species, there was an extension of the distance between the input and output regions on our brain. Due to this structural advantage, when we see a stimulus, we know it does not have to lead to automatic response.[5] Better yet, we have time to use the input in a creative or controlled way that often times leads to a more unique and healthier output. Because of our larger space between these two regions, we can allow ideas and other inputs to marinate in a sense; to be swirled around and mixed with other already-present ideas, forming something original and different in the process. We are the only creatures that are able to use our mind to first imagine and then create. A human can look at a desolate, bare piece of land and turn it into a fertile, prolific garden by simply employing imagination and creativity. Humans go beyond the instincts of survival, capable of pausing to think, in order to not just survive but thrive.

Going beyond the difference in minds, think about an eagle's nest. Does an eagle build its nest on the ground with twigs and grass? Not any eagle I've seen. They chose a prime location up high in order to see everything that comes and goes. Now, relate this back to your mind. Do you stimulate your mind in order to be more conscious of what you are putting into it? What you are spending most of your time thinking about? Do you practice the art of autosuggestion, voluntarily injecting or rejecting thoughts based on their ability to serve or destroy you?

---

[5] The Creative Brain by Dr. David Eagleman

These are questions with answers that have a direct impact on your chances of success or failure. Take the time to stimulate your mind with healthy emotions, like faith, love, and hope, in order to set your mind up for positive thought production. In doing so, you will prepare your conscious mind to send positive vibrations to your subconscious. Not only will this impact your overall character for the better, but the universe will recognize your thoughts that are mixed with faith, love, and hope and send you the physical equivalents of these thoughts.

Go back to the eagle's nest. We know that it is built up high (often 70 ft off the ground), but what about the materials? Eagles don't bother adding weak twigs and moss to their nest. Remember, this is their home. This is where they create their future through the production of young. Your mind is the same. It is where you create. This is the one place where you can have complete control.

The eagle choses the strongest and sturdiest of branches, sticks, and foliage to construct its masterpiece. In this way, the nest remains sturdy and sound, and eagles often add to the nest year after year. Because of this, nests can often grow to be quite huge. In fact, according *Beacham's Guide to the Endangered Species of North America*, one nineteenth century nest in Ohio measured 12 ft (3.7 m) deep and 9 ft (2.7 m) in diameter.[6] Your brain can be expanded likewise. You can continually construct, renovate, and fortify it with uplifting ideas and profound knowledge. Only allow thoughts of a constructive and positive nature to enter into your subconscious.

At the same time, there are instances when we have to defend our minds from invading thoughts and our laziness. eagles keep their nest in tip-top shape, repairing any damages as soon as possible. Any invaders looking to steal eggs or cause a disturbance are sent away with passionate declarations from the eagle. You must learn these tactics of defense. Show no mercy to those negative and depressing thoughts that try to enter the gates to your subconscious. Strike them down and

---

[6] "Bald Eagle." Beacham's Guide to the Endangered Species of North America. Encyclopedia.com.

replace them with positive reassurances and suggestions. Construct your mind with thoughts that will make a solid foundation to prepare you for the harsh storms life will throw your way. Be prepared but also remember to never get comfortable. Remember that storms will keep coming to test the sturdiness of your mind. Without proper care, the foundation trembles. Grow your mind and build upon it.

Many people wander through life and let thoughts come and go as they please. Some actively seek sources that give rise to thoughts of a destructive nature. The author of *The Alchemist*, Paulo Coelho, once wrote, "Most people see the world as a threatening place, and, because they do, the world turns out, indeed, to be a threatening place." If you could see inside these people's brain, you would only see a nest barely held together with duct tape and dust from the trampled ground. Don't be like these individuals. Decide to take a stand and become master of your thought-horizon. Once you start to control how you think, you can start to control what life will present you with.

People who complain all the time are almost always negative thinkers. They are always the victims. They couldn't do this because of that. They couldn't go there because of that. They spend so much time thinking of excuses that opportunity and life passes them by. If only they would put as much focus on getting the task done as they do coming up with excuses, then maybe they would get somewhere. Don't be a complainer. As Author and Minister Francis P. Martin puts it, "Do not ever confess, 'I'm tired.' What good will that do you? If you feel tired, just say, 'my strength is renewed as the eagles.'" He couldn't be more right. When we complain about things, it does more harm than good; we are allowing ourselves to be convinced we have no control. However, when we reaffirm ourselves and ask for strength during trying times, we can convince ourselves we have control over the situation and will come out just fine. We also can look to the following Bible verse from the prophet Isaiah:

> Did you not know? Had you not heard? Yahweh is the everlasting God, he created the remotest parts of the earth. He does not grow tired or weary, his understanding is beyond fathoming. He gives strength to the weary, he strengthens the powerless. Youths grow tired and weary, the young stumble and fall, but those who hope in Yahweh will regain their strength, they will sprout wings like eagles, though they run they will not grow weary, though they walk they will never tire. Isaiah 40: 28-31 [7]

When you feel that life is pushing you down and the negative thoughts begin to creep in, ask God to help you sprout wings like those of the eagle's' so you can fly free from worries and despair. Ask Him to empower you so you can soar with faith and love toward your future accomplishment Ask Him to renew your tired spirit with a fire that will stop at nothing until it has burned through life's tiresome barriers. Adopt the mindset of an adventurer. When bad things happen, accept it as a building experience and move on toward your goal with an optimistic spirit.

Many of the difficult times in our life leave the greatest impact on the development of our character. Consider Matthew chapter 7, verses 13-14: "Enter by the narrow gate, since the road that leads to destruction is wide and spacious, and many take it; but it is a narrow gate and a hard road that leads to life, and only a few find it."[8] Our brains have been historically primed by the comforts of traditional society to often times take the path of least resistance in order to better ensure our survival. But in this day and age, those who want to change the world can't be afraid to take risks. True leaders see the narrow gate as a welcoming challenge, something that will surely be more uncomfortable, but they

---

[7] https://www.bibliacatolica.com.br/new-jerusalem-bible/isaiah/40/

[8] https://www.catholic.org/bible/book.php?id=47&bible_chapter=7

know it will also prove to be much more interesting. They adopt an explorer-like spirit and scout the path ahead, searching for things that will test them and add to their life's insightful experiences. The love of adventure and the faith of inner-growth, keep them on course. It can't hurt to think positive when things aren't going your way. It can only help; and it will, as long as you mix these thoughts with powerful emotions, such as faith.

Faith is the emotion that gives energy and life to the thoughts that are sent into the world. Without faith, there would be no way to create things. Everything starts out as an idea, a thought. To bring a thought to reality, one needs to have faith. To have faith is to believe something without seeing it physically. You've got to hold an image in your mind of the kind of person you want to become and then act with full confidence that your transformation will take place. You know the saying, "Fake it until you make it"? Within reason, this phrase holds tremendous value if you can apply it in your life when you need to psych yourself up to become that person. Most people think faking something or being someone, you're not is immoral. It certainly can be, but for our purposes here, it a prime way to change ourselves for the better. Change starts from the inside out.

To change our life, we first have to change ourselves. We have to change our way of thinking. "Faking it", or masking ourselves with a desired role, begins the transformation process. You almost have to fool your subconscious by consistently telling yourself that you are that person with those qualities inside and out. It may seem foolish at first, but sooner rather than later, your subconscious will accept these suggestions and follow orders, bringing every physical thing that matches with that role into your life as a byproduct.

Now, it's time to ask the three famous questions, starting with WHY. Why should I follow the Law of Attraction? Well, if you want to do some great with your life, if you really want to create something grand, if you really want to serve the world, if you really want to be a better person, it all starts with conquering your mind. A man who has no control over his thoughts has no control over his life, and in turn, has no control over his future. Another WHY question to ask at this point is why don't more people know about this law? And better yet, for the people who do know, why don't they use it to their advantage? The answer has never been found. Sometimes there is no way to explain things. It's tough because many times people who know this information try to help others they care about by spreading the word, but sadly, the message only reaches the soul of maybe one out of ten people. We simply don't know why that is. Just be glad you now know this information and can use it to build a strong and steady nest designed to withstand the onslaught from life's wind of pestilence, a nest constructed of the finest thoughts which serve to create the perfect environment for the generation of ideas, a nest you defend with unmerciful tact against all inputs and thoughts that seek to destroy.

So how will you go about applying this Law of Attraction? The best place to start is by continually reminding yourself of your tremendous self-worth through personal affirmations. An example of a positive affirmation is something as simple as telling yourself, "I matter. I am confident and more than able to achieve my goals." Set reminders on your phone or computer to remind you it's time to reaffirm yourself with positive statements spoken both inside your brain or even better, speaking them out loud to hear, as this increases the tendency of embedding them into the subconscious. Aim to do this at least three times a day. Slowly, saying your personal affirmations will become a habit and you won't need the phone/computer reminders anymore. Repeating these affirmations will boost your confidence and allow you to concentrate more on *life-giving* thoughts than *life-taking* thoughts. It will also be a nice break throughout the day, which can help you relax and meditate in your own world for a bit. Before you return to the complicated and sometime hectic community, your strength will be renewed and you'll be ready to tackle any problems with a positive and victorious mindset.

Need a real-world example of how it's done? Just consider arguably the greatest American president of all time, Abraham Lincoln. Honest Abe wasn't born with a silver spoon in his mouth, and most of the world saw him as nothing more than a poor boy on a dirty farm. But he had a different way of thinking than most. Young Abraham lost his mother to disease and later his sister to childbirth. He also lost his first love, Ann Rutledge, to typhoid. One of his sons, Tad, died in a carriage accident while Lincoln was president. All of these terrible tragedies, Lincoln not only endured but overcame. Not to mention being a leader in the midst of a warring, divided nation, having to sacrifice his time and energy to commandeer the country through the perilous storm. The odds definitely seemed to be stacked against him.

However, Lincoln knew victory is born in the mind. He had a natural love of reading and brought books with him wherever he went, which injected bounds of knowledge and ideas into his growing mind. He also had an art for storytelling, and was able to use this advantage to reach prime political positions and eventually the White House, even after earlier devasting defeats for the Senate. But Lincoln understood his advantages, and used his mind to spell victory for his cause, which was a united and equal nation. Even after many defeats and setbacks, he stayed true to the Law of Attraction and refused to become pessimistic. Instead, he harnessed all the positive affirmations he could and began to work on the solution. Lincoln knew if there was a mind willing to commit itself to its idea of victory, it would happen. For this reason, America became a once again united nation, stronger and more unified than before, and freedom was establishing for millions of slaves. Lincoln knew exactly what his mission was on this Earth, and he knew exactly how to attract it into its physical form—by positive-attracting thoughts.

"Every man is said to have his ambition," Lincoln wrote, "I have no other so great as that of being truly esteemed by my fellow men, by rendering myself worthy of their esteem. How far I shall succeed in gratifying this ambition is yet to be developed."[9] Because Lincoln had this deep desire, he attracted the things that would challenge and test him to make important decisions that would directly impact the nation and its men and women. At times, he had to deal with dissatisfied men, but only for the greater good of the nation. Lincoln is one of the most noted presidents because he had attracted growth and development by placing his energy and thoughts toward the fulfillment of his ambition, and he changed the world in the process, etching his name into the history books with all the other legendary men willing to put the weight of the burden upon their leading shoulders to create an entirely different and finer domain.

And now WHAT. What will change for you as a result of following the Law of Attraction? For one, you'll notice negative things slowly dissipating from your life and other, more positive things waking up to greet you in your daily life. Instead of seeing the negative side of things, you'll have a more optimistic outlook toward life. People will be attracted to your elated attitude and desire to be in your company. The most important thing that will change is the structure inside your mind. All of the weak, rusted, negative ladders and slides will be wiped out and replaced with strong, reinforced positive ladders and lifts. Your mind will have a whole new way of thinking, a way designed to produce in exact form what your ultimate desires are. You'll become a magnet, pulling your dreams and objectives closer to you with every powerful thought. There is so much to be excited about when you begin to actively change your entire way of thinking into neat, organized systems which only serve to improve you and help see your goals through to fulfillment. One of the best parts is that once you get into a habit of thinking this way, it will be hard to go back to your old behavior of just aimlessly letting your thoughts wonder. You'll be too busy smiling from the results to even consider your old style of "thinking". Not only will

---

[9] "Team of Rivals – The Political Genius of Abraham Lincoln" by Doris Kearns Goodwin

your smile be brighter but you might even see your shadow dance in the sunshine brought on by your very thoughts.

Take a look around you. Everything around you has been attracted to you and brought into existence on account of your thoughts, your mind. Now ask yourself if this is where you want to be in the next month, year, or decade's time. If not, then start today by attuning your thoughts to serve your purpose and define your life. I'll leave you with this quote by Plato: "The first and best victory is to conquer self. To be conquered by self is, of all things, the most shameful and vile." Command your positive thoughts to conquer and subdue the negative. Control your destiny by controlling your thoughts.

Chapter 4

THE LAW OF WEALTH

Money is finite. The mind is not. Use the mind first and the money will come in responsible fashion.

> "Your financial requirements or wants have nothing whatever to do with your worth. Your value is established entirely by your ability to render useful service or your capacity to induce others to render such service."
> – Napoleon Hill

There are a few men sitting in a room full of cash. Piles and piles of it. Stacked up to the ceiling. They could be doing anything they ever dreamed of with the money, but they are just sitting there. They are hungry. They are thirsty. They are stressed, and they are not happy with their situation. How could this be, you ask? It will become very clear when I tell you who these men were.

Pablo Escobar and his Colombian drug front pulled in an insane amount of cash. Through illegalities backed by acts of violence, they kept Colombia under their brutal control for much of the 80s to early 90s. The nation was practically torn apart by drug wars, mercenaries, bombings, and assassinations, not to mention having a reputation as a cocaine country. Columbia is still struggling to shake this off. All of these terrible things, just so Pablo and his drug lords could stack their money.

Think how this relates to the first part of the story. Pablo and his men had all of this money, but they couldn't leave the room in fear of being killed or captured. This illustrates an important lesson. Money cannot save you. Money cannot make your problems go away, no matter how much of it you have. The only thing that can aide you in your troubles is wisdom. Pablo and his posse knew how to make money on an illegal basis, but because of their lack of wisdom, they didn't know how to create wealth. They only knew how to make money illegally, which is certainly unwise, so they found themselves helpless in a room full of money simply because they didn't have the wisdom to know how to create wealth legally and profitably without having to look over their shoulders the whole time. They focused on *taking* things from others and surviving off the resulting turmoil and weaknesses. A true leader focuses on what he can *give* the world. Only then can he achieve the wealth he so rightfully deserves.

This brings us to the formula for creating wealth. Wisdom + Money = Wealth. Where do you get the wisdom? A great way is from studying books about wealth and listening to advice from the wealthy. Once you have the wisdom, you can always make money, no matter how many times it is taken away from you. Remember the lesson from the last chapter about your mind, your nest? This is the center of all creation. If you invest knowledge into your mind, it is bound to create things of a similar nature.

Being wealthy is not just about having money. Being wealthy means you have the unending ability to create income. Let's look at the life of the eagle. Of course, there are no forms of money throughout the avian world (not that I know of at least), but there are important resources of value, such as young, territory, and prey or food. The eagle has the built-in instinct to know how to create and defend these resources. If they happened to be taken away or die, the bird would continue to carry on and create more of these resources. Its survival as a species depends on it. You have to look at your life in the same way.

Nobody is born wealthy. They may be born into a family with lots of money, but this doesn't make them wealthy, only rich. Wealth is like a skill that must be practiced in order to see the benefits. No one comes out of the womb knowing how to invest their money responsibly. The process of becoming wealthy takes time, and mistakes are necessary, and even encouraged, in order to learn. To become wealthy, you cannot fear the loss of your money and resources; you have to take each setback as a welcomed lesson that provides you with more experience and knowledge to use for your future financial decisions. Taking risks is a part of the learning process. There is a difference, however, between blind risks and educated risks. Blind risks are taken without any thought or reflection and are usually decided out of desperation or fear. Educated risks, on the other hand, have been thought out carefully and are decided out of knowledge and faith. Use your past experiences, your brain's ability to make connections between various ideas, and your support system of friends, family, and experts in order to take educated risks.

If you want to be wealthy, one of the first steps is to learn from others' past experiences with the subject through books or other resources. I have some suggested reading at the end of the book to help get you started. But maybe you're thinking "Why do I want to be wealthy?" That's a great first question. It can be answered by following process detailed below.

First, it's necessary to establish the required wisdom, then let it take the reins of your financial decision making, guiding you into a wealthier future. A lot of people say "Well if I had money, I'd know what to do with it." Do you think that's what the eagle says when breeding season comes? "Well if I had a chick, I'd know what to do with it." You know that's not the case. An eagle does what it was born to do and creates young to ensure a future. Like an eagle, you must study what you need to create your wealth and mold your future, not only for you, but for your future generations. This is it. This is why. You want to be wealthy not just to ensure your well -being, or even your family's well-being; it's much more than that. You want to ensure your future generation's well-being. And not just by creating money, but by setting a strong example as a wise and wealthy leader who took great care to set up his or her future generations for survival and success. You want to go into the night knowing that you did your absolute best to provide for yourself, your family through the years, and your community.

People get it mixed up. They think it's all about how much money you make. But it's not how much money you make. I'm sure you know, or have heard stories about, people who have great high-income jobs and are still struggling to keep up with the basic necessities of life. So it's not about how much you make. It's about *what you do* with how much you make. It's all about learning how to manage your resources. One of the fascinating things about an eagle is that it knows how to balance its resources to better serve itself and its future. When it hunts for prey, it doesn't always kill the animal and gobble it up That would not be using eagle Vision to look towards the future. The eagle instead saves much of the food for its chicks. It keeps enough in its own stomach to keep it going, but no more than this. It knows that it needs to give the proper amount to its young to ensure their bright future.

Eagles have a peculiar advantage when it comes to storing their resources. Their esophagus is equipped with something called a crop. It essentially allows them to store up to two pounds of food whenever food is quite abundant.[10] This means that when the difficult times come (and they always do), and food becomes scare, an eagle it can go several days without needing to find new prey by feeding itself from its crop of stored food. The eagle has prepared itself during the good times and uses what it has put away to survive.

---

[10] Peter E. Nye , New York State Dept. Environmental Conservation, Division of Fish, Wildlife and Marine Resources, Albany, NY ; https://journeynorth.org/tm/eagle/facts_characteristics.html

As humans, we aren't built with this advantageous anatomy of food storage (although we do have Tupperware), but we can learn a valuable lesson from the eagle's method of preparedness. Essentially, by keeping resources stored for safekeeping, whether that be food or money or education, we can rest easier knowing we are more prepared for when challenging times come to test us. I remember my wife telling me once that it is always a good idea to have at least three months' worth of rent in a savings account just in case one loses his or her job and needs time to find another occupation.. When we capitalize when things are going well, we ensure we will be better prepared when life's waves come to clean the beach. It's okay to build the sandcastle, but it would be wise to construct a castle a little farther up the beach too, out of reach of the cleansing tidal waves.

American Author George S. Clason hit the nail on the head when he wrote "Wealth that comes quickly goeth the same way. Wealth that stayeth to give enjoyment and satisfaction to its owner comes gradually, because it is a child born of knowledge and persistent purpose." People who hit the jackpot or come into money quickly are not likely to grow in the world unless they have the wisdom that comes from gradual study. Pity these people because without knowing the Law of Wealth, their shares of money will melt away like a snowman in the warm sun, like we have seen time and time again.

So here comes the second question. If you can't spend all of what you make on yourself how, then do you distribute the money? The answer is simpler than you think. It can be summarized as such: learn to live off 70 percent of your income. Less if you can, but without needing to get some cardboard box beds. When I say "live off", I mean being able to pay the things in your life that are necessary to survive decently. Things like rent, utilities, food, and water—he essentials. When you live at a lesser means, and don't adjust your lifestyle to your incremental raises in income, you incrementally save more and more. In other words, the 70 percent stays the same in actual numerical figures (such as $25,000, for example) but your 30 percent numerical figure grows as your income grows. This means that your savings are growing while you are living the same lifestyle. It can be tempting to adjust your habits to your new income and/or savings, but stay disciplined and resist. You will be doing important things with this 30 percent. Your personal savings, emergency funds, investments, and, perhaps most importantly, donations will all come from this 30 percent. You will be surprised how much you can get out of so little.

Let's look at the one of the richest men in the world, Bill Gates, creator of the multibillion-dollar company Microsoft, and a true pioneer and leader in the software industry. As much money as Gates has acquired over the years, hardly ever do you see him using it wastefully on things that only bring temporary happiness. Yes, he occasionally treats himself to some simple joys in life, but, overall, he doesn't change his spending habits based off his growing income. Just look at a picture of him and his clothing style. Not a Gucci belt or Rolex in sight, at least in the pictures I've seen. What most people do is spend their money on material things as soon as they can in order to validate themselves to society and give the appearance of being rich. They adjust their spending habits as their income increases so they always stay in the same place in life or, even worse, go down into a hole of debt.

Gates recognized the material things that money can buy mean nothing if you haven't got the wisdom to manage your resources. Just look at the proof of Gates' spending habits and you will clearly see why he does all of this; why he chooses to serve the world. Remember that the WHAT is the proof or result of your WHY or your belief. Bill didn't do it all for the money. He knew the money would come eventually if he only kept his mind on his goal of changing the world and making software more accessible for the common man. He wasn't motivated by money. He was driven by his deep desire to change the world. Gates may have once kept much of his income to himself, but his outlook on life completely changed when his mother passed away from breast cancer in 1994, which came just after his marriage to Melinda French. After this, Bill and Melinda decided to renew their perspective on the world and travel. Soon they started a family, and with Melinda's influence, Bill became interested in philanthropy work, following the civic leadership role set by his mother. He studied the way Andrew Carnegie and John D. Rockefeller, two of America's greatest industrial titans who donated money to important worldly causes. It was then that Gates knew he had a responsibility to give more of his wealth to a charitable and higher cause.

In 2000, the couple combined several family foundations and made a $28 billion contribution to form the Bill & Melinda Gates Foundation.[11] The foundation now contributes its resources to addressing various international and domestic issues ranging from public health to children education. Because Gates decided to use his wealth wisely, he is doing something much more valuable and rewarding than simply working at Microsoft. He is leading by serving others in need. And rightfully so, his grave will be exhalated and remembered long after his death because he believed in something bigger than himself. By focusing on how we can be of service to others, we increase our ability to think creatively and deliver a service of value to the world, in turn attracting equal sources of value, such as money and assets, into our lives as a result of our contribution.

The best leaders lead by serving their fellow man. They are not focused on the reward, the money, at least not primarily. No, they have the wisdom to recognize that first they must render themselves as effective servicemen, staying focused on their belief of how they can change the status quo through selfless commitment and service. Then and only then, do the rewards come. It doesn't work the other way around. Service must come before the money, or better said, before the wealth.

This same selfless behavior of eagles as parents can help explain why these magnificent birds continue to survive even in light of today's increasing threats to its habitat. Mother imperial eagles, for example, choose to feed their offspring before feeding themselves. They put the

---

[11] https://www.biography.com/people/bill-gates-9307520

future of their very lineage first before giving in to their egocentric, self-preservation urges. Humans can learn a valuable lesson from this. If we first feed (deposit money into) our savings or our future (our offspring and lineage) before feeding ourselves (our irresponsible and selfish spending habits), then we ensure our continuation and future success. Mother eagles instinctually know how to prioritize their life in order to increase the chances of their offspring. After the eaglets have had their fill, the Mother eagle will come back to the nest to feed herself, however, if the eaglets show any sign of continued hunger, she will immediately stop and let her young eat undisturbed.[12] We can apply this seemingly basic knowledge to our daily lives by developing the wisdom to know when to allow our future savings, investments, and assets to accumulate and grow without interfering with them by giving into our selfish wants and/or presumed needs. It takes practice, it takes discipline, and it takes self-control. In order to evolve our level of awareness, we need to prioritize our entire life around the future of our existence and keep our thinking centered around this philosophy for every decision we make.

It's easier said than done, and I know it's easier to say all this stuff than it is to actually do it. Just know that I am human and that I'm working on this stuff equally as you. I know the temptations of life. I know the feeling of missing out on something fun because of the need to save. Sometimes I give in to these feelings of instant gratification and spend my money on things that don't last, but afterward the feeling of regret usually sets in and I remember how important it is to stick to this law of wealth and ensure my family's future.

I will say one thing though about giving into the different types of temptations. I classify them into two types, materials and experiences. Materials can be anything from a nice dress to a fancy car. You are

---

[12] "Imperial Eagle, Aquila Heliaca, A Pair of Imperial Eagles Five instincts" A documentary by Leonidas Presinsky, Press in SKY, 2003; Additional credit to Richard Galas, Stanislav Prokes, Stephen Michael Bradford, Ivan Prikopa, Anton Strecky, and Frantisek Pic.

usually thrilled right after you buy them, but soon enough, the "new car smell" fades away and you notice the purchase only created a feeling of temporary happiness. Happiness can't be bought. "Happiness is just a moment before you want more happiness," said Donald Draper from the AMC hit show *Mad Men*. I believe happiness comes from our experiences in life. Examples of experiences could include fancy adventures like traveling to a remote beach in Europe to something as simple as taking a walk in the park with a loved one. Each of these experiences make memories, and the money spent on making those memories is better spent than the money spent on a simple possession that will lose its novelty in a few weeks. Memories never lose their power to stimulate deep feelings of emotion. So, in short, if you have a choice to spend your hard-earned cash on a material or an experience, choose the experience. Nine time out of ten it's the less selfish and more profitable decision for all parties involved.

So, the last question. What will happen if I follow this Law of Wealth. The answer: you will change for the better. Yes, your bank account will change, your money habits will change, and your entire lifestyle will change, but the greatest thing that will change is your mind. Your mind will increase in priceless value only by studying the wisdom behind wealth. This is the real treasure. Not money. Money can always be made, but wisdom, once absorbed and understood, can never be taken away.

An eagle's spirit will never be broken. If its wing becomes damaged, maybe it will die, but one thing is for sure, it will continue to try – to try and fly. It will hold the belief that it can continue on and soar towards the heavens. And sometimes, when its will is strong enough, a miracle will occur and lift the eagle upwards. Our life can be seen in the same way. Our materials, our money, our resources can all be broken and lost in a terrible tragedy or circumstance, but within our mind we have the ability of pressing on by the sheer determination and braveness that comes from the knowledge that these things can all be made over 1,000 times after they are lost. Once we hold the wisdom of wealth, we have the power to create these resources and materials, regardless of how many times they are lost or taken from us. Put simply, once an ability is learned and practiced, it can never be forgotten. An eagle still knows how to fly, even if its wing is broken. After studying wealth, you will know how to become wealthy, even if your bank account is broken. Knowledge is the real value here, not the money it brings. Be like the eagle and let your spirit never be broken when all seems lost, for remember that with your mind properly prepared, you can create and recreate anything infinitely. The potential is yours forever, once you have the knowledge; you just have to use it properly by serving others. This is the secret to true wealth.

Chapter 5

Parkinson's Law

Leveraging for success when time is short

"Success requires no explanations. Failure permits no alibis." – Napoleon Hill

British naval historian by the name of Cyril Northcote Parkinson once wrote an essay in 1955. In that essay, his first sentence read as this: "Work expands to so as to fill the time available for its completion." The core of this statement can best be summarized in the following example. Imagine you have a project due a week from now. During the coming week, you have worked intermittently on the project and by Thursday, one day before the due date, you feel like it's almost complete. Then something unexpected happens. Your computer crashes and you lose all the work. You become frantic. Almost all of us know this feeling. After your initial freak-out, you try to organize your thoughts.

Are you going to have to tell the professor what happened and hope for the best? You could, but that would only be an excuse, and eagles don't give excuses, only results, despite the circumstances. Instead you decide to close yourself up and focus intensely for the next eight hours. You know it's a hassle but you also know this is life's way of testing you. It's how winners and losers are separated. Losers usually give in at the first sight of outside forces closing in. Winners overcome these forces and bravely take on all responsibility, using the power they have to fuel them to the finish line.

Let's explore the first question again: WHY. Why should you use this law? Well, let's look at another question which might help you see it clearer. Do you see why it would be unwise to complain and give excuses when the unexpected happens and your time is cut short? Parkinson's Law is on your side, if only you will employ it when applicable. Not only can you use this law when surprises occur, but you can also use it proactively. By setting short deadlines for yourself, and having the discipline to keep them in place, you can arouse your brain into a state of crucial concentration and focus. The task at hand stands no chance to a person with this mentality. By shortening the deadline of your own tasks, projects, and responsibilities in life, you create a more productive atmosphere to not only complete the objective but add to it with brilliancy and precision, something which might be more difficult to do when using the original deadline which allows you more time to get distracted by minor things.

People often wonder how this differs from procrastination. Procrastination is purposefully delaying something due to laziness or lack of desire. When you use Parkinson's Law, you act today instead of delaying something, and you use a shorter time limit to help you fix your thoughts into a more productive form. Think back to the eagle example, the king of the sky. Do you think this bird became a predator at the top of the food-chain by delaying its objectives until the last minute? Most certainly not. That would go against its primal instinct. The eagle takes advantage of Parkinson's Law by acting as soon as the stimulus shows itself. Its energy (work) grows to fuel itself in completing the search for food, a mate, or territory. Likewise, there is a special reserve of energy inside each of us which only reveals itself when stressed by outside forces that threaten our survival. By employing Parkinson's Law, we tap into this hidden energy reserve and use it to our advantage.

This hidden energy reserve principle is used constantly in the world of exercise and heavy lifting. I remember doing P90X during my senior year of high school. (P90X is a ninety day training DVD program you can do at home.) Tony Horton is the lead trainer and creator of the program, and he sure knew how to get you involved and make the workouts feel more engaging. In between all of Tony Horton's dad jokes and intense motivation, I heard him quote some very intriguing and agreeable ideas. One thing is always said was, "Do your best, and forget the rest." What a great statement. If we can block out all of those excuses and circumstances and only focus on how we can give it our all, then are we not using the maximum capacity of our characteristic energy supplied to us by the one and only God? Horton said another thing that really stuck with me. I don't remember the exact wording, but he said something like this: "Most people give up and stop doing the exercise when it starts to feel uncomfortable. The trick is to try to do three more reps when the tension and irritation sets in." I see this is where there's the greatest chance for progress. Whether you are bench pressing, doing push-ups or some squats, pushing yourself past the natural feeling of discomfort is how we push our boundaries and expand our abilities. By using our hidden reserve of energy, we can sculpt our minds, bodies, and spirits into a form that reflects total dedication and absolute control.

Now, how can you use this principle? Start implementing it slowly with minor things. Give yourself a short deadline to do an errand or chore around the house. Set a short-term goal and hold yourself to a schedule without relying on excuses and complaints when something unexpected happens. After you begin to show mastery of the application of this law to minor tasks, you can use it in more influential areas of your, life such as your work, relationships, health, and finances. Everything that has a known task, in every area of your life, can be subjected to this law for increased energy and increased focus.

Let's look back to one of the oldest examples of this law found in the book of Exodus. Most of us know the story of Moses and how he led his people, the Israelites, out of Egypt with the help of God Almighty. There is something spectacular in the way the Israelites left that attests to Parkinson's Law. Because the Egyptians had finally had enough of the plagues and now feared for their lives, they actually drove the Israelites out of Egypt, giving them fine jewelry and clothing in the process. Since there was no time to plan, Moses and his people had to essentially take what they could and seize the opportunity to be free from oppression. They weren't sure where they were heading, but they knew where they were coming from. They knew that if they wanted things to change, this was the time.

Exodus 12: 39 - 41 reads:

> And with the dough which they [Israelites] had brought from Egypt they baked unleavened cakes, because the dough had not risen, since they had been driven out of Egypt without time to linger or to prepare food for themselves. The time that the Israelites spent in Egypt was four hundred and thirty years. And on the very day the four hundred and thirty years ended, all Yahweh's armies left Egypt. [13]

The Israelites had no time to linger. Because they didn't waste their time and instead used the scarcity of time to seize the moment, God ushered them across the Red Sea and destroyed the Egyptians following in the process, ridding the Israelites of their oppressors. They lived in Egypt for more than four hundred years, and, in one day, the whole course of their history took a turn toward the promised land of milk and honey. Many Christians still honor this ancient tradition by using unleavened bread during Sunday Communion.

God spoke to Moses soon after the Israelites' journey out of Egypt. Exodus 19: 1-6 reads:

> Three months to the day after leaving Egypt, the Israelites reached the desert of Sinai. Setting out from Rephidim,

---

[13] https://www.bibliacatolica.com.br/en/new-jerusalem-bible/exodus/12/

they reached the desert of Sinai and pitched camp in the desert; there, facing the mountain, Israel pitched camp. Moses then went up to God, and Yahweh called to him from the mountain, saying, "Say this to the House of Jacob!" Tell the Israelites, "You have seen for yourselves what I did to the Egyptians and how I carried you away on eagle's wings and brought you to me. So now, if you are really prepared to obey me and keep my covenant, you, out of all peoples, shall be my personal possession, for the whole world is mine. For me you shall be a kingdom of priests, a holy nation." Those are the words you are to say to the Israelites.[14]

This passage reminds us how God watches over us with everlasting love and mercy, and keeps us riding on the wing of an eagle toward light and fulfillment, though only if we trust in Him and drop everything when He calls us to act. When we confide in God, no task is impossible. When time seems short, remember this story and how God rewarded the Israelites for acting in great haste, in turn deeming them as His personal possession, His holy people. A nation, that with God, would be free from worry and fear brought on from time constraints. A nation that would recognize no such thing as stress. A nation that would breathe with faith knowing that God was on their side during the good times as well as the bad.

There are many things to learn from this story of Moses and the freedom of his people, but in our case, we can focus on recognizing the value of knowing how to act promptly and decisively when given a fixed amount of time. Using the "healthy stress" created from a short-time stimulus, we can trust in God to hold us on course and work to complete our task successfully. In this way, we confide in God and don't rely on easy excuses and alibis. We rise to the challenge and trust

---

[14] https://www.bibliacatolica.com.br/new-jerusalem-bible/exodus/19/

in ourselves. Anyone can think of a reason not to do something. Be the person who steps up to the given circumstances and resolves to accomplish the task or die trying. Both outcomes are considerably more rewarding than giving up.

What will happen after trying the law out? You will begin to see that, instead of dreading to start tasks with long deadlines like you were before, you will begin to embrace the intense energy burst and concentration that comes when you give yourself short deadlines. You'll be increasingly more productive, doing bigger and better things in smaller increments of time.

The eagle knows how and when to use its energy reserve. You must not be reckless and set an impossible deadline which only will exhaust you and disrupt your work and progress. Start small. Kick back the hours a little bit and try it from there. Then, when you start to get the hang of it, you can challenge yourself further by setting progressively shorter deadlines. It's important to know when to stop, though. We have other things we need to tend to in our life too, things that don't pause to our deadlines and set priorities. With these, step back, adjust, and then get back on course after tending to these important things. An eagle knows its limits as well as when to turn its attention from its task to something of a higher priority, such as its mate or chick, essentially its future.

To summarize, sometimes things happen in life that are out of our control. We are presented with a choice when this happens. We can either cry and complain, cite it as an excuse for where we are in life and watch opportunity fly by, or we can embrace the challenge, tap into our energy reserve and adjust our flight pattern effectively, stopping at nothing until the task is complete. The second option is chosen by all those who want to capitalize on opportunities to grow. We only grow by difficulty, not by staying comfortable. Create the discomfort and hold your focus to a challenging time limit, fueling yourself with energy reserves which take you right to the door of opportunity. Remember this quote from American author, George S. Clason: "Opportunity is a haughty goddess who wastes no time with those who are unprepared." As the eagles do, fly with a fixed eye and never taking it off your target. Apply Parkinson's Law and you'll be well on your way to maximizing your productivity and increasing your opportunities for growth.

Chapter 6

THE LAW OF VIGILANCE

Conformity assists in your survival; except when it doesn't

"Where we all think alike, no one thinks very much" –
Walter Lippmann

A s we go about our daily lives, we do many things without thinking about them. Breathing, walking, yawning, just to name a few. The less time we spend thinking about doing these things, the more time we have to think about things of greater importance, such as school, work, family matters, etc. This ability to automate things has contributed much to our relatively exponential advancement and evolution as a species. Imagine if you had to think about putting your foot down each time before you take that next step. It would be a headache just to walk around the block. Our brain has evolved to do this type of thinking for us automatically so our conscious can think about other things that are less habitual and more challenging. It is quite a spectacular tool which has taken us to many heights of achievement as a species.

As advantageous as this automation is, there is one disadvantage: When our brain is on autopilot, we are more susceptible to being influenced by persuaders. We act without thinking and may do something we never truly wanted to do. This happens because we are relying solely on our inner autopilot and past experiences to guide us in every decision that crosses our path. In most cases, our autopilot makes the right decision and we continue to survive and thrive. But in some cases, the situation calls for more conscious thinking in order to escape the prowls of unwanted influence.

Let's look at an example. If I came up to you on a street while you were walking and gave you a flower and then asked for you to contribute a donation to my foundation, church, or whatever, would you agree that you would be more likely to give me a donation just because I gave you the flower? As humans, we feel an inner urge to reciprocate a gift that is given to us. This is because we don't enjoy the feeling of being indebted to others. Psychologically speaking, we feel more pressure to return a favor because the fear of feeling guilty grips our brainstem and tells us to get even and reciprocate the act of charity. So when someone presents you with a free gift, be wary and ask yourself if it is really a free gift or a sales tool?

This is just one small example of persuasion and influence that happens every day. There are many more examples and principles that I could write about, but for the sake giving you immediately usable information, I only want to introduce the fundamentals. There are entire books devoted to the psychology and principles of persuasion, and I will suggest some further reading at the end of this book. Here is a short list of advice I've followed to help you defend yourself from influences that may alter your course:

1. Before you agree to anything, always consult yourself and ask "Is this something I really want or need in my life or am I feeling inclined to do (or buy) this because of an outside influence or favor, which would in actuality be a sales tactic?" Learn how to politely but firmly decline offers.

2. Ask yourself if the thing you are interested in is only interesting because of its variable difference in comparison of something else. For example, a rock appears heavier than it actually is when

you lift it right after lifting a bag of feathers. The same rule works with anything. If you just had a whole bunch of salty popcorn, of course you're more willing to pay for a refreshing drink. Pay attention to pricing in stores and comparison methods sales-people use. Say a you were just shown some of the worst houses in town by your realtor and then they finally show you a halfway decent home at the end of the day. You will of course be inclined to think that it's much more attractive than it actually is, because you are comparing it to the terrible houses you just saw. It's a tricky and effective strategy.

3. When you decide to do something because of an attractive factor, ask yourself if you would still decide to do it if the attractive factor was removed? When people commit to something, they have a tendency to continue and follow through, even if the original thing that interested them is removed from play. Car salesmen use this and it's called "low-balling". An example could be that you were excited about this car that had a state-of-the-art brand-new leather interior. The salesman and you spend some minutes discussing other features and you're in the office looking over the contractual paperwork. The salesman then informs you *sadly* that they unfortunately don't have the model with the leather anymore, only cloth. Because you've been there for an hour or more and initialed half the paperwork, you feel much more inclined to go ahead and go through with it, because you feel like you've already committed; even though the feature that you really wanted and attracted you in the first place, was removed from the deal. The salesman built all these other pillars around you to hold you up, and then carefully but swiftly dragged the main column (leather interior) out from under you; but you were still supporting the offer because of the other pillars built up in the process. Look into it this selling method and be wary.

4. People tend to look around them and chose how to respond to situations by observing other people. This can be helpful or harmful depending on how the interpretation it's used. Be cautious when you are subjected to information when in a crowd of people; don't spend too much time observing and imitating. Act on your own accord.

5. When you start to feel like you like a salesperson, be cautious. They may have been using techniques to make you more comfortable with purchasing or doing something to their advantage. Make your decisions based only off the deal itself, not on whether or not you like the presenter.

6. When figures or subjects of authority present themselves, before you submit, ask yourself if this authority is really an expert or if are they only pretending. Also ask if they have any reason to be untruthful. These questions can save you from buying a product or doing something because of what a false expert says or does.

7. When things become limited or are presented as scarce, we tend to want them more, even though we don't need them in the first place. You'll see this used in marketing all the time: "Get in while supplies last" or "Limited time only." It's best to remember that the actual nature of things don't change when they appear to be limited. And many times the offer or item comes around again, or something better does.

To put it simply, turn off your autopilot every once in a while and ask yourself if this is really what you want or need to do. It's impossible to live without our autopilots, but we can train our brains to be more aware of situations that require conscious thinking in order to conquer the pressures of influence and make choices on our own terms without being taken advantage of. Robert B. Cialdini, PhD, said it best in his ingenious book *Influence: The Psychology of Persuasion*: "With the sophisticated mental apparatus we have used to build world eminence as a species, we have created an environment so complex, fast-paced, and information-laden that we must increasingly deal with it in the fashion of the animals we long ago transcended." So, although we need this older style of survival-thinking, we must not become lost in it. Sometimes we have to think more instinctually than automatically in order to get the most out of the situation.

In the open sky, the eagle can turn on auto pilot and cruise, allowing it to fly freely while focusing on other things. When having to fly through a crowded forest with branches and obstacles, though, it switches into manual mode and brings greater attention to its wings and velocity. Like the eagle, you have to learn how to recognize the open sky from a crowded forest. That is to say you have to know how to judge situations as either autopilot appropriate or autopilot inappropriate. It's then you have to know how to grab the gear shifter and take the controls yourself, maneuvering around influences and getting to your destination with your values intact.

Now to our favorite question: WHY. Why should you learn to be vigilant? Again, looking at another question to help us answer this. Do you want to be like a feather in the wind, drifting from one persuader's breath to another? With this behavior, you are less in control and more subject to being taken advantage of. Not only that, but you are less valuable to your fellow human beings because of your aptness of being manipulated. When you are vigilant, you are in a state of high focus. It is an invigorating feeling to be awake enough to say, "I am at the controls and I will decide whether or not I want this."

Many people make the mistake of subjecting themselves to inputs that don't serve their best interest. Zig Ziglar, the famous motivator, said it best when he stated, "You are what goes into your mind." What we decide to subject our eyes and ears to essentially seeps into the base of our minds, close to the control panel where it can influence our future decision-making process. When we watch reality television or the news for example, we have to be extremely careful of how much time we spend absorbing this information simply because of the negative effect it can have in our lives. It's alright to have limited exposure to these types of reasonable sources, but we must be careful to keep it under control and not allow ourselves to become influenced by these societal factors of how life should be.

Exposure to other sources have more extreme consequences. Inputs such as porn, strongly-worded music, crude movies and TV shows, and other destructive media can create an unnatural disharmony in our lives. Even worse, these subjections can become addictive and spur a downward spiral of negative thinking and depressive behavior. The best way to combat these sources is by replacing them with more self-serving, positive inputs. These are essentially defined as the opposite of the bad sources, like positive, inspiring books, movies, and TV shows. Consider listening to a good, uplifting album of your favorite band or a walk in the woods accompanied by the sounds of nature and peace. Remember their positive associations, especially if they are practiced habitually, eventually become positive bonds which then become positive foundations for your mind to build upon. This is why some people's minds can be compared to a sturdy structure built upon study rock, never faltering when the heavy storms come. Others' minds are built on soft sand and wither away when the clouds release their fury. Jesus shared this with us more than 2,000 years ago when He said,

> Therefore, everyone who listens to these words of mine and acts on them will be like a sensible man who built his house on rock. Rain came down, floods rose, gales blew and hurled themselves against that house, and it did not fall: it was founded on rock. But everyone who listens to these words of mine and does not act on them will be like a stupid man who built his house on sand. Rain came down, floods rose, gales blew and

struck that house, and it fell; and what a fall it had![15]
Matthew 7: 24-27

It's a fact of life that the rains and storms will always arrive. Think of it as a way of keeping life interesting. The key is to strengthen our minds in order to be better prepared for when these harsh torments come. We can do this by injecting our minds with positive, natural medicines that stimulate the positive emotions in our soul: faith, love, joy, etc. These medicines can be found just about anywhere; we only have to have the discipline and wisdom to subject ourselves to them repeatedly in order to ride out the storms which test our strength and principles that make up the foundation of our minds.

We must keep our minds attuned to actively decide what we will subject them to every day. Sometimes, in today's complicatedly connected world, it's impossible to willfully keep our minds completely closed off to all bad sources. In these cases, we must rely on our reserves of already absorbed positive elements, using them to combat the wicked subjections and eventually overcoming the virus that persists in trying to hack into our mainframe. Beat such evil back by placing yourself in your brain's captain's chair and steering your mind toward the healthy and joyful thoughts which can block out the bad.

But how to apply the Law of Vigilance? Where do you start? You start by learning about our human psychological tendencies. It doesn't take long to learn our inclinations and patterns of behavior once you make yourself aware of them and press them into the subconscious of your mind. Then use this information to aid you when you're flying through the crowded, influential, worldly forest. Learn how to recognize that feeling in the pit of your stomach that tells you that you really don't want this, you just feel *inclined* to want it. With continued practice, you'll see your awareness and sensitivity to detecting influences

---

[15] https://www.catholic.org/bible/book.php?id=47&bible_chapter=7

will grow to become a formidable wall which protects you from being preyed upon by clever foxes.

One of the best allies on your journey of practicing vigilance is patience. Patience will keep you calm and release any pressure you feel when you're put into a situation that tugs at your instincts. Work on developing patience in order to give yourself time to think before committing to something. Let the world wait a moment; it is your life and the decision is nobody's but yours. People may think it strange that you take some time to think, even with the simplest of decisions, but do not let their lack of understanding deter you from seeking the best possible outcome, which can only come from conscious thinking. Do not be lazy and procrastinate, but do not be hasty and impetuous. Work to find the proper balance between decisiveness and careful consideration.

And this leads us to the WHAT. What will happen after following and employing the Law of Vigilance? For one, you'll find that your confidence will raise to an ultra-high level on account of your ability to continually arrive at the destination you want on your own terms without the feeling of guilt from unwanted acts or purchases. Heighted confidence effects everything positively in your life and, believe me, people will notice your difference in demeanor. The Scout motto is Be Prepared. When you are vigilant, you show the world that you are indeed prepared.

Chapter 7

THE 80/20 LAW

The Ratio that keeps on keeping on...Follow it to better things

"You simply can't think efficiency with people. You think effectiveness with people and efficiency with things." - Stephen R. Covey

When working on a work project or school task, have you ever completed everything with perfection down to the last detail, overworking yourself in the process, only to notice the supervisor or grader paid attention to a small portion of the project/task before deeming it satisfactory? It has happened to almost all of us. We put so much work and sweat into something and, at the end, we come to see that only a small part of the finished product was responsible for the successful presentation.

There is a deeper meaning behind this, a law actually, that was introduced in 1896 by Italian economist, Vilfredo Pareto. The visionary noted the famed 80/20 connection while at the University of Lausanne, and published it in his first work, *Cours d'économie Politique*. He came to this realization after performing an experiment with his pea plants in his garden. Pareto noticed that only 20 percent of the pea pods in his garden were responsible for 80 percent of the peas. This can be generalized to mean that 20percent of one's input or work produces 80 percent of the output or product. Pareto applied this principle to many areas of life; one most notably was the conclusion that 80 percent of a nation's income was in the hands of only 20 percent of the population. His specific illustration being that 80 percent of the land in Italy was owned by 20 percent of the population. Here are other examples that also may peak your interest:

- 20 percent of criminals commit 80 percent of crimes

- 20 percent of drivers cause 80 percent of all traffic accidents

- 80 percent of pollution originates from 20 percent of all factories

- 20 percent of a company's products represent 80 percent of sales

- 20 percent of employees are responsible for 80 percent of the results

- 20 percent of students have grades 80 percent or higher

Going back to our project example before, the small part we could have mostly focused on more was this 20 percent, which was in in turn responsible for 80 percent of the effect the project gave. This means that if we had put most of our efforts on this 20 percent, then we would have saved many hours of overwork and exhaustion while still securing good praise from the supervisor.

The 80/20 Law can be applied everywhere in our lives: school, work, relationships, investments. You name it. There is a special 20 percent that is responsible for 80 percent of the results in all of these areas. If you want to see the majority of growth, you have to find the minority responsible. This is not being lazy or counterproductive. It's called working smarter, and it will save you tons of time. This is not to say the other 80 percent of input is not important; it still holds value and has its place in the effectiveness as well. The law only invites us to place more focus and emphasis on the more influential 20 percent factors that directly correlate with the majority 80 percent results.

Pareto's principle has generally only been referenced in the in the personal and social aspects of society, with its general claim that 80 percent of the outcomes of interest are often due to 20 percent of the possible causes or individuals. More specifically, it is often applied in the field of management and economics, drawing off Pareto's original claim that 80 percent of the wealth in Italy is owned by 20 percent of the population. Recently, however, we have seen evidence that this principle not only applies to humans, but can also be witnessed in the animal kingdom, more specifically with birds. The Royal Statistical Society performed a thirteen-year case study watching and noting the various types of birds seen in two specific territories. The first territory, called Brookhaven National Laboratory (BNL), was rather small, only making up 8.23 square miles. The second territory, called, New York State (NYS), was on a much larger scale, occupying an area of 54,000 square miles. After analyzing both sets of data, the Society found a reoccurring theme: 80 percent of the birds that were seen belonged to 20 percent of the species that were seen. That means of the roughly 125 different bird species noted, only a relatively small percentage of the species (~20 percent) accounted for a large percentage of the total observed bird population (~80 percent).[16] Look at the table below to see how surprisingly close these numbers are to the classic Pareto 80/20 ratio. The Pareto Principle doesn't seem to be restricted to only the human community.

---

[16] "Even birds follow Pareto's 80–20 rule" case study - Fred J. Rispoli, Suhua Zeng, Tim Green, Jennifer Higbie; published: 19 February 2014 - The Royal Statistical Society

Year	Percentage of BNL population from top 20% of species	Percentage of NYS population from top 20% of species
2000	73%	81%
2001	77%	81%
2002	76%	80%
2003	80%	80%
2004	77%	81%
2005	74%	80%
2006	79%	81%
2007	75%	81%
2008	77%	80%
2009	74%	80%
2010	71%	81%
2011	73%	80%
2012	76%	80%

(Data each year during the period 2000–2012, identified the 20 percent of the species with the largest populations at the Brookhaven National Laboratory (BNL) and New York State (NYS) sites, and then determined what percentage of the total population is due to the top 20 percent of the species.)[17]

What can this trend tell us? One thing is that people are not the only ones who operate by this law. The world is a competitive place. We

---

[17] Table 1 of "Even birds follow Pareto's 80–20 rule" case study - Fred J. Rispoli Suhua Zeng Tim Green Jennifer Higbie; published: 19 February 2014 - The Royal Statistical Society

often forget this in our world of comfort and security. It appears that the animal kingdom, and birds more specifically, demonstrate that the most successful species of the kingdom come down to approximately 20 percent. Looking past economic and other elements of study, we can come to the same conclusion, stating that the most successful people in the world are those few in the 20 percent. Just simply knowing this can be of tremendous value. If only around 20 percent of the population is successful, that means there is something they are either doing or refraining from doing that keeps them ahead of the majority 80 percent. The idea is to follow the practices and the trails blazed by these few. It's easy to do what most everyone else is doing and become another sheep. However, by doing this, you're only conforming to the life of mediocrity. Study what the small minority of achievers are doing and see if you can apply it to your lifestyle. As Mark Twain once said, "Whenever you find yourself on the side of the majority, it is time to pause and reflect."

So why adhere to this law? Why not put all your elbow grease and sweat into the entire project? The answer is quite simple: to save time and energy and to focus on what really matters in order to use your time more creatively. The 34th president of the United States, President Dwight D. Eisenhower, once said, "What is important is rarely urgent, what is urgent is rarely important." Ponder this for a moment. Combining this statement with Pareto's law, we can surmise that 80 percent of all the urgencies that present themselves are unimportant and can usually wait. Responding to emails, making unnecessary revisions, renewing your programs, and other busy work seem urgent but often times they're not important. What is important are the more creative tasks such as constructing a presentation, writing a short story, designing a new space, or other things that give you a real sense of joy and fulfillment. If you are working yourself to the point of exhaustion by unconsciously responding to any stimulus that's calls for urgency, it's actually counterproductive because there is only so much your body and mind can take before collapsing from overexertion. In addition, you're taking time and energy away from your potential to create something meaningful. Stimulants, like coffee and energy drinks, will only work their magic for a short time, plus they can wreak havoc on your health. Save your energy for something that unleashes your mind to explore. Do something more relaxing or creative. Spend it with your family playing a board game. Try your hand at painting. Do something that makes you smile.

Eagles have a special technique when flying that helps them save energy. It's called soaring, and it is much more energy efficient than constantly flapping their wings. They use thermals updrafts to their advantage and allow themselves to glide over the landscape at a steady speed as they hunt for food. Prey can be quite scare at times, so eagles often have roam the skies, essentially waiting to see signs of any prey. Until then, they want to use as little energy as possible. This is parallel with the 80/20 Law. 80 percent of an eagle's success depends upon the 20 percent of energy it use while soaring. It's an astounding principle when you think about it.

Next question. How can you start using this law? The easiest way is to first identify your desired results in all areas of your life. This can be done by looking at what has been produced so far in terms of all the areas of your life: health, school, family, spiritual, profession. Where do you stand now? And how did you get there? Then ask yourself if it has pleased or displeased you. If it has been pleasing to your life, write it down. If it is displeasing, write it down as well. Compile a list of all of your positive and negative outcomes. Once this is done, trace the outcome back to the start. What input helped create this product or result? Now, and this is the important part, decide to cut the inputs out of your life that either aren't producing desired outcomes, are wasting too much of your valued time, or are using too much of your needed energy. For the last part, circle the few, stand-out inputs that contribute to most of the desired outcomes that are healthy in terms of time and energy use. If you have done this process right, you will have just identified the special 20 percent that is responsible for 80 percent of your success. Let that sink in for a moment while you feel your tension slip away.

And now for the WHAT. What will change after applying this law? For one, you'll notice you're a lot more cheerful because you've organized your life. By turning most of your focus to the prime 20 percent, you'll have a lot more time to simply enjoy life and be happy, basking in the shade of your 80 percent tree, grown from the smaller but proliferous 20 percent roots. You'll be more effective at solving problems and have more time to think and act when the unexpected happens on account of all the time and energy you'll have stored.

An eagle makes a living off of smart, energy-efficient hunting. It survives by saving its energy until the crucial moment of diving on its prey and carrying its weight back to the nest. It's wise enough to know that going full speed at all times is a crash course with over exhaustion and eventually failure. To be more effective, be more efficient with your energy and time. Follow the 80/20 Law and soar your way to the target.

Chapter 8

THE LAW OF PERSISTENCE

Channel the spirit within you to keep at it, after you feel all but beat.

"Practice isn't the thing you do once you're good. It's the thing you do that makes you good." – Malcolm Gladwell

Picture this. You're in a cave hunting for treasure. Its dark. It's cold. You've been searching for hours on no sleep. You're not sure how much longer the cave continues, but you're also not sure you want to continue. It is at this moment that a very important choice comes across your mind: give in and go home, telling yourself it was a good try, or suck it up and continue on, staying on course. The vast majority of people would choose the first option and go home empty hand. There are a select few who know something the majority doesn't: the Law of Persistence. This is what carries them onward to the treasure they seek, even after challenging obstacles and temporary failures. These few know these minor setbacks and defeats are not permanent. They actually don't see them as defeats or failures. They see them as tests, tests by mother nature to gage our passion towards our objective. If we are not passionate enough, we give up and do something else. If we let our passion fuel us through the difficult times, however, then we pass the test and move closer to our objective. Author and Bluefish CEO, Steve

Sims put it frankly when he wrote, "No one ever drowned from falling in the water…they drowned from staying there."

The Law of Persistence says that, if you are moving toward something, you will have to prove yourself by overcoming obstacles and setbacks that test your actual level of focus and desire to achieve your goal. You see, nature does not favor those who want something lightheartedly. Nature takes sides with those who prove they want something with all their heart and will stop at nothing in order to succeed. Think of it as a "weed out" course in college. For those of you who don't know, a weed out course is a very trying and challenging class that everyone in that particular major must take and earn credit for in order to graduate. An example for a biology major would be biochemistry or organic chemistry. These both have the reputation of pushing students to their limits and effectively remove the "weeds" (students who can't cope with the pressure) so that by the end of the class, only the "flowers" (the passing students) are left to continue their track to become a doctor, medical scientist, etc.

In reality, courses like biochemistry and organic chemistry, although both important, may not have any information you'll be readily using when you continue on in your studies and career. This is how these tests are sometimes. In some cases, they do not appear to directly correlate with your mission or objective. But there is a hidden, buried cable that indirectly communicates with your end goal. We cannot say that something is not important if it is not seemingly relevant to our main task. Remember that everything matters and that everything effects everything.

Some tests are not as obvious as the ones taken with pencil and paper. Sometimes life sends an undercover agent to find out how much we really want something. If our focus isn't strong enough, we only see an insurmountable burden and give up, letting failure overtake us. Yet, if we continue to try with unshakeable determination, only two things can happen: we achieve our objective or die trying. The King's Guard in ancient Greece held a special motto: "All men have fears, but the brave men put down their fears and go forward, sometimes to death, but always to victory."

These are the two options which make nature a beautiful and also challenging force that engenders both gratefulness and respect. What is important to remember is that it is equally glorifying to perish in pursuit of one's destiny as it is to achieve it. Great leaders know their life is not permanent but the effects of their actions can shape the world into a new place far longer after they are gone.

Eagles are driven by the Law of persistence every moment of their lives. They are only successful in procuring prey in one out of five hunts. This means that 80 percent of the time, they fail to capture their objective, the food that will keep them as well as their future generation going. Imagine the determination and strength of their mind that tells them to keep going until success. If eagles weren't persistent, the wouldn't control the skies. Far from it, they'd be on the ground like the majority of animals, burrowing and living perhaps an easier, more comfortable life; comfortable, that is, until they're swooped up to supply the need of a higher player in the food chain. Pope Francis made a remarkable speech in Poland for World Youth day in July 2016. His message tackles the problem of comfort and security the world is experiencing today.

"Dear young people, we did not come into the world to 'vegetate'.... We came for another reason: to leave a mark," said the pope. "The times we live in do not call for young 'couch potatoes' but for young people with shoes, or better, boots laced." Pope Francis also warned of a "harmful and insidious paralysis" that comes from "confusing happiness with a sofa. A sofa that promises us hours of comfort so we can escape to the world of video games and spend all kinds of time in front of a computer screen....A sofa that keeps us safe from any kind of pain and fear."[18]

The point is that life isn't supposed to easy and comfortable. It isn't supposed to be hard and uncomfortable all the time either. Rather, life

---

[18] https://www.telegraph.co.uk/news/2016/07/31/the-world-has-no-need-of-couch-potatoes-pope-tells-young/

is meant to be challenging and rewarding. With persistence, we break through the difficult barriers and establish a new, wider comfort zone, which allows us to see farther along the horizon. And, after accomplishing this breakthrough, the reward is more enjoyed and feels more deserved. When we reward ourselves without doing the work, it feels selfish and superficial. Eagles capture their prize by persisting even in the face of failure. They know with each failure, they are closer to success. They are aware their lives are not as important as the knowledge they leave behind for their future eagles. This is why their species lives on, changing their world for the better in the process.

Rearing young is perhaps the most stressful time for eagle parents. The mother must stay with the nest to provide protection while the father scans the landscape fervently looking for food for his family. They will often alternate parental jobs and each will take their turn staying with the young and hunting for food. The amount of stress and work would be enough to topple the relationship had the eagles not developed a close connection from the beginning. In fact, scientists and researchers have seen evidence of eagle partners participating in intercourse not solely for its role in reproduction but also at times to reduce stress. This is not to say that we as humans should have intercourse with anyone at any time to reduce stress (please, we won't even go there). It is to illustrate the immense connection the eagle partners have with each other, which enables them to be effective parents in the most stressful of times. This bond is not easily made, and its history involves perilous steps and maneuvers that the eagles use to demonstrate their love and devotion.

The death spiral is perhaps the best example of one of these bond-locking maneuvers that bald eagles engage in. The maneuver is chief among their "spectacular courtship rituals," says wildlife ecologist David Buehler of the University of Tennessee. "The two soar up to high altitude, lock talons, and tumble and cartwheel toward Earth." They let go before reaching the ground.

The courtship display is about "'determining the fitness of your mate and making that mate want to mate with you,' Buehler says. 'It's like going out on the dance floor if you're a really good dancer.'" There are risks: the stunt could, for instance, end in a fatal crash. "'It's an interesting tension,' he says, 'between succeeding with a mate and maintaining your own survival.'"[19] This is just another way of saying that eagles value the feeling of love over the fear of death. Love often makes us do irrational things, but by controlling this feeling of passion, we are able to drive out the fear of death and fuel our love for life. Even simple acts of kindness toward each other can help us push onward in trying times; especially if the acts are spontaneous and unexpected.

In the case of imperial eagles, the female is the larger of the sexes, as with most types of eagles. Her size and strength may appear intimidating superficially, but the female eagle does not use these traits by bullying or bossing her mate; quite the contrary. She instead focuses on capturing larger pray which can provide more food for her mate and her family. And what does she do in the moment she brings the pray down? She chooses to feed her mate first before herself. She actually places the flesh in his mouth, servicing him even though she is physically stronger and bigger. She is a leader because she serves. She is *persistent* in showing her partner love and support because she knows that they are stronger and more likely to preserve over obstacles together when they help to keep each other at their best. She recognizes that her mate's smaller size also has advantageous, allowing him to hunt with more speed and agility. She is *persistent* in showing her partner love and support because she knows that they are stronger and more likely to preserve over obstacles together when they help to keep each other

---

[19] "For Amorous Bald Eagles, a 'Death Spiral' Is a Hot Time" by Patricia Edmonds
https://www.nationalgeographic.com/magazine/2016/07

at their best. Together, they value their strengths and work together to mate, hunt, and defend their territory. [20]

Eagles are monogamous birds and mate for life. They stay hitched until death do they part. These birds know partnership is not easy but they know that with their solid resolution of true commitment, they are pressing onwards towards higher skies. They don't give in at the first signs of stress or failure. They instead learn to stick it out and become stronger in the process. We can learn a lesson from this. Marriage, for example, should never be seen as easy. It takes work and devotion. Once you win over your spouse, you can't say that's it and never do anything else to remind him or her of your love. You have to continually win them over and continually show your devotion. What's the best way to do so? By being able to stare at the face of death without fear, to love so much that you are willing to die for your mate. This power of love is what leaders can use and have used to change the world.

Martin Luther King Jr. believed in the equality of all races and knew his life was at stake when committing himself to this cause. Gandhi believed in a free country with harmony among its many various believers and knew his task was worth more than his life. Jesus is the greatest example. By willingly giving His life away, His teaching of unconditional love and faith have lived on for more than 2,000 years. These great leaders changed the world because they were persistent with their efforts and only let faith dominate their mind; they drove away any fears and doubts from the onset.

When we fear things, whether it be the outcome, the pain, or the even the loss of our life, we enslave ourselves to the curse of comfortableness and stillness. In other words, we forgo our ability to change the world by unwavering faith in persistent action. It's important to note that worry is a natural survival instinct which has helped us survive

---

[20] "Imperial Eagle, Aquila Heliaca, A Pair of Imperial Eagles Five instincts" A documentary by Leonidas Presinsky, Press in SKY, 2003; Additional credit to Richard Galas, Stanislav Prokes, Stephen Michael Bradford, Ivan Prikopa, Anton Strecky, and Frantisek Pic.

as a species. We have learned not to do certain things for the fear of pain or death. As a survival aspect, this is important, and we need this power as much as we need the power of faith. But let it not be misunderstood: the power of fear will come to dominate our mind and stop our progress if we allow it. Fear is worry at its highest level. We need to learn how to let worry help us by acknowledging it in our mind as only advice; that we can take note of and not give any more attention to it. If we begin to dwell on this worry, the seed grows into a tree of fear. When this happens, all progress is stunted. Instead, we need to plant the seed of faithful, positive thoughts that, with the proper persistence of attention, will grow into a tree of faith, guiding us towards our objectives with grace and elation.

Anything that you now fear has to be replaced with the feeling of faith that you will get where you are going. Any images you hold in your mind that feed your fear must be permanently substituted with images that feed your faith. By *persistent,* conscious thinking, you will either rise or fall, depending on which thoughts you allow to dominate your mind. There is no reason to fear death. We are beings made up of only matter (our bodies) and energy (our spirits/minds).

The first law of thermodynamics states the total amount of energy in a closed system cannot be created nor destroyed (though it can be changed from one form to another). If this is the case, when we die, our energy doesn't disappear. Instead, it lives on in another form. Although our body may decompose, its matter doesn't dissipate into thin air, it only changes form into smaller particles to feed and nourish the earth (if we're buried for example.) The point is that death is not the end. It is merely a transition. A way of changing our shape into another form of service to the universe. Don't fear the grip of death or it will slow any progress you attempt to make in living. On the other hand, don't seek death rashly and take unprecedented risks. You must tenaciously live the life you were given to the best of your ability and smile when your time comes, knowing you did all you could with the time you had. When it's time to change your form of energy and matter, be optimistic that you'll be able to serve the world with the same level of selfless and unwavering character.

Now for our first question: WHY. Why follow the Law of Persistence? The answer depends on who and where you want to be in life. Do you want to follow your dreams, your destiny, your desires and change the world for the better? If so, you'll need to know right here and now that it won't be an easy road and there will be many trying barriers to test your passion and determination. Only by practicing the Law of Persistence can you overcome these obstacles and move towards your goals.

One of the best examples of a man who employed the Law of Persistence is Thomas Edison. Born in 1847 in Milan, Ohio, Edison's future didn't look too bright (pun intended). The youngest son in a family of seven children, Edison was different from the beginning. One of his teachers deemed him "difficult" for his hyperactivity and his tendency to be distracted. He also had a bit of a hearing problem from a series of ear infections and a claimed "train incident". At first glance, it is easy to say that from early on, the boy's odds did not appear to be stacked in his favor. However, Edison's youth did have a silver lining. His mother, Nancy, influenced much of her boy's thirst for knowledge. She was a successful school teacher and taught Edison mostly at home, encouraging his curiosity and eagerness to learn in the process.

Edison had very little formal schooling, only attending for a few months at best. Despite this, by the age of thirteen, he got a job selling newspapers and candy on a railroad line. In his free time, he read many scientific and technical books, and even learned how to operate a telegraph machine, a recent invention that was revolutionizing the communication industry. At age sixteen, Edison landed a job as a telegraph operator and grew his mind in parallel with the industry. From here on, Edison began to develop his first inventions and receive his first patents. He began with an electric vote recorder, a device intended for use by elected bodies such as Congress to speed the voting process, however,

Edison failed to gain the public's popularity and it was a failure.[21] So what did the man do? Did he throw in the towel and go back to his day job without another thought of creativity? No, not Edison. He knew that with this defeat, he was now closer to success.

Many successful inventions followed, which gave Edison fame and fortune, including the Universal Stock Printer, the tin foil phonograph, and motion pictures to name a few. Not to mention the vast laboratories he built, which transformed the scientific and research architectural world, providing a blueprint for future effective laboratories to be constructed all across the nation. Still, the inventor had failures during this time, including his attempt to develop methods of mining iron ore to feed the insatiable demand of the Pennsylvania steel mills. Edison could never make the process commercially practical and it ended in disaster, with a total loss of investments and capital acquired from selling his shares of General Electric stock.[22] Of course, Thomas Edison's most famous invention, the incandescent light bulb (which was actually an invention that was not new; Edison only made it safe and practical for home use by perfecting it), was not successful until he overcame a large number of insufferable defeats. The writer Napoleon Hill, who knew Edison very well, wrote about his friend's persistence through his many failures in his great book, *Think and Grow Rich*. One of the best quotes reads, "Thomas A. Edison 'failed' ten thousand times before he perfected the incandescent electric light bulb. That is – he met with temporary defeat ten thousand times, before his efforts were crowned with success."

Many of us can hardly imagine failing ten times at something and having the determination to continue. Failing ten thousand times is daunting to read, but the success that came afterward engenders more hope and restores more faith than any degree of fear or frustration steaming from the fire of these numerous failures. Thomas Edison had

---

[21] https://www.nps.gov/edis/learn/historyculture/edison-biography.htm

[22] https://www.biography.com/inventor/thomas-edison

such an admirable level of persistence that drove away any thoughts of doubt or quitting. Life rewarded him for this courage, and now he is recognized as one of the best inventors of all time. He changed the world, and literally brought light to our homes and to our lives.

How can you practice this? How can you persist in the face of failure? The next time a test presents itself, ask yourself if your objective is worth more than the pain of going through this test. If yes, then you are reassured that the feeling of accomplishing your goal will be far greater than the feeling of enduring a painful test of faith. Be persistent with your thinking and continue to reaffirm yourself that it will all be worth it in the end. For example, start setting small goals at first and brainstorm possible obstacles that will or could jump onto your path. Determine your passion toward these goals by accessing your willingness to go through the obstacle. This is also good for narrowing your focus and letting your mind concentrate more on the things you really want, the things that really drive you. Once you have determined your most important and passionate objectives, move on to developing the habit of repeating positive affirmations to yourself during seemingly idle and difficult times along the journey of fulfillment.

And finally, the WHAT. What will change after following the Law of Persistence? You'll notice your amount of focus and ability to readjust your direction toward your goals will increase immensely. You'll have increased levels maturity and self-control to make it through the storms of life, and come out stronger and closer to the mountain top. You'll see you are starting to become a force of nature that stands up to the tests and perseveres, even in the dimmest of light. Your defense and armor will be made of the finest elements, causing any striking sword to break into pieces and leaving your attackers stunned as you continue you seize upon the walls blocking your path to your destiny. Your hope and confidence will not be flaunted by the temporary defeats and failures. Instead, you will be strengthened because you know, that like the eagle, you'll be one step closer to your glorious victory.

Conclusion

That brings us to the end of this book, but also to the beginning of your journey. You now have the knowledge necessary to successfully navigate the world in search of your purpose and passion. I ask that you don't simply put this book down and let it collect dust. Pick it up every now and then to let your brain marinate in its message. I also encourage you to dive deeper into the realm of personal development. Don't stop here. Look into each of the laws shared and find books more specific to that particular principle. I have listed some good books to start with. Remember, you don't have to read them all at once. Just start with one and commit yourself to a small page limit of ten to fifteen pages a day. Like a steam train, little daily habits are sometimes difficult to start, but once they have some steam behind them, they're very difficult to stop.

Many questions have been posed in this book, but they can all be summed up into one question: are you an eagle or a pigeon? Pigeons live off of the scraps others drop or leave behind. Eagles pursue their cause with a victorious mind. What you become starts in your mind. Eagles make it their underlying purpose to live life on their own terms, above and out of reach of the more simple-minded animals subjected to circumstances and scavenging for food in order to survive. A great majority of humans are like the pigeons that populate their cities and live off their crumbs. But there are the persistent few that rise from the shallows of the city streets and become independent creatures that create their own future on their own terms. Eagles take the path of difficulty because it brings more opportunities to grow, and they then pass that strength on to their future generations and fellow brethren. Eagle decide to hunt not just because of what they get out of it. No, no. They decide to hunt because of what they become in the process.

Life is a curious mystery in and of itself, and those who know the laws and apply them discover the astounding benefits and privileges that life has to offer. Those who disregard these laws and live in ignorance go through life like a bouncing beach ball, being tossed up and down by the wind and the surf.

I'd like to share one of my favorite quotes about the meaning of life from the Infamous playwright George Bernard Shaw:

> This is the true joy in life—that being used for a purpose recognized by yourself as a mighty one. That being a force of nature, instead of a feverish, selfish little cod of ailments and grievances complaining that the world will not devote itself to making you happy. I am of the opinion that my life belongs to the whole community and as long as I live it is my privilege to do for it whatever I can. I want to be thoroughly used up when I die. For the harder I work the more I live. I rejoice in life for its own sake. Life is no brief candle to me. It's a sort of splendid torch which I've got to hold up for the moment and I want to make it burn as brightly as possible before handing it on to future generations.

You have to look at your journey in the same way. Don't think about what you are getting out of life. Think about the type of person you are becoming during your daily actions. Are you becoming a stronger, more capable, independent human being every day? Or are your actions making you into a dependent pessimist who can't catch a break. You've got to understand that eagles don't catch breaks or wait for good luck. They simply set a task and follow it through without complaint or steering off course. Louis Pasteur once said, "Chance only favors the prepared mind." Commit yourself to these Eagle Instincts and you'll soon be soaring through the skies, fulfilling your dreams and becoming better every day, in every way.

Suggested Reading

I can't tell you the right books to read; I can only tell you what I've read and how I got started. Here, I will tell you which books are the most important and should be read at all costs. There are five must-read books I will devote a paragraph to in order to explain them in further detail; the others I will list by book title. One note here: I recommend buying all of your books if you can. Try not to borrow books from friends or get them for free because it will feel like less of an investment in yourself. When we pay a price for something, we automatically value it more than if we receive something for free. When we invest our time and money into something, we are more likely to stick with it and apply the things we learn, simply because we have given some of our resources in order to see its fulfillment. So buy the book. Most won't be over twenty dollars, and the return of investment will be tenfold if you understand and apply the lessons seriously.

The Five MUST- READ Books

1. *The Slight Edge* by Jeff Olson

As I said before, my personal development journey started with *The Slight Edge*. I highly suggest starting with this book because it will teach you the first law, the Law of Time—discipline. After reading and applying the principles laid out by Olson, you will develop the discipline to continue your personal development journey. This book should come first because it gives you the proper fuel to continue reading. Without first learning discipline, it'd be tough to keep reading book after book. Discipline is like the GPS that guides you toward your destination. To get somewhere, you have to start by knowing where you are going, and *The Slight Edge* is a great book to spark your thinking about your goals and how to develop the proper discipline to get you there.

2.   *The Alchemist* by Paulo Coelho

This a such an enlightening read which really makes you reflect on what it is you want to get out of life. Paulo Coelho tells the story of how a young man searches for treasure in the desert and how what he learns along the way completely changes him and his place in the universe. For all those who have dreams and desires, this book is essential. By reading it, you will have a better sense of how to gauge your life's compass. Your direction in life will be less obscure, and you'll start to think with great energy and determination about what it is you want to do and who you want to become.

3.   *The Richest Man of Babylon* by George S. Clason

This is the one book of wealth that has long been the "go-to" for all those financial masterminds. Written in the early twentieth century, *The Richest Man of Babylon* is composed of insightful parables and scenes from the ancient Babylonian civilization, which was famous so many years ago for its riches, hanging gardens, and formidable fortress. Clason teaches us the laws that make up the backbone of all things to do with money. It's an enjoyable read with lessons in almost every paragraph, so have your highlighter ready to carve out your favorite lines from this classic staple of wealth literature.

4.   *How to Win Friends and Influence People* by Dale Carnegie

This book teaches you exactly what the title says. Carnegie lays out the fundamentals and the techniques for handling all different types of people and situations you'll encounter in the world, especially in the workplace. Your whole outlook on people is likely to change completely after studying this book. You'll learn the motives behind people's actions, including your own, and how to control the impulse to react negatively to unfavorable circumstances, using instead the impulse to work in your favor. Anyone can benefit greatly from this book, no matter what line of work you're in. As for politicians and corporate employees, this book should be sewn into your blazer.

5. *Think and Grow Rich* by Napoleon Hill

If there is one book that can uncover the formula for becoming rich, this is it. Becoming rich isn't just about money; it's about growing rich relationships, a rich health regime, and rich inputs of stimulation, among other things. Napoleon Hill organizes this book into fifteen chapters, thirteen of which are steps proven and designed to help the reader grow rich. The chapters vary in length, but most contain around twenty to thirty pages of the book's total 371 pages. This book was published in 1937, right after and during some of the darkest recession years America has ever seen. The reader can almost feel Hill's sympathy for the broken-spirited American people, and he writes to them with strong words of encouragement and motivation. Napoleon Hill found his destiny when Andrew Carnegie advised him to create a clear, accessible resource for all that focused on the combined steps and philosophies all the great leaders and rich men employ to take them on the journey to success. He writes with words that reveal the insight and thinking of some 500+ successful and rich men and women at that time. This book is on another level, and I suggest reading it after first reading five to ten other books about personal development, only because *Think and Grow Rich* is very profound and deep. After many paragraphs, I found I often had to stop and really ponder a sentence, presented example, or story. This book delivers the framework for all those who want to be successful.

Additional Reading

1. *Who Moved my Cheese?* by Spencer Johnson

2. *Rich Dad Poor Dad* by Robert Kiyosaki

3. *The Dreamgiver* by Bruce Wilkinson

4. *The Tipping Point* by Malcolm Gladwell

5. *Blink* by Malcolm Gladwell

6. *Hung by the Tongue* by Francis P Martin

7. *Bluefishing* by Steve Sims

8. *Start with Why* by Simon Sinek

9. *The Compound Effect* by Daren Hardy

10. *The Business of the 21st Century* by Robert Kiyosaki

11. *The Business School for People Who Like Helping People* by Robert Kiyosaki

12. *The 21 Indispensable Qualities of a Leader* by John C. Maxwell

13. *A Technique for Producing Ideas* by James Webb Young

14. *One Minute Manager* by Kenneth Blanchard Ph.D.

15. *The Magic of Believing* by Claude Bristol

16. *Managing your Day to Day* by 99u

17. *Outliers* by Malcolm Gladwell

18. *I Wear the Black Hat* by Chuck Klosterman

19. *Confessions of an Advertising Man* by David Ogilvy

20. *Influence, the Power of Persuasion* by Robert B. Cialdini Ph.D.

21. *Team of Rivals: The Political Genius of Abraham Lincoln* by Doris Kearns Goodwin

22. *The Four-Hour Workweek* by Tim Ferris

23. *The Seven Habits of Highly Effective People* by Stephen R. Covey

CPSIA information can be obtained
at www.ICGtesting.com
Printed in the USA
BVHW071259170123
656442BV00007B/879